TRAINING FOR ENDURANCE

*Guide for Endurance
Athletes of All Levels*

The information contained in this book is from the author's experiences and is not intended to replace medical advice. It is not the intent of the author to diagnose or prescribe.

Before beginning any program you should consult with your physician, and address any questions to your physician.

Case studies in this book are those of real people whose names have been changed to protect their confidentiality.

Editor
Hal Walter

Cover Design
Kathy Capp

Cover Photography
Swimmer: Steve Tarpinian, president and founder, Total Training Inc., www.swimpower.com
Runner: Bill Coppel, president and co-founder, MAF Group, www.philsbar.com
Mountain biker: Corbis Images

Typography
Out There!

Printed in the United States
Library of Congress Catalog Number: 00-133002
Second edition

ISBN: 09642062-7-7

David Barmore Productions
P.O. Box 250, Todd Road
Stamford, NY 12167

*For all who seek endurance
and optimal human performance*

Table of Contents

Foreword

Train slower to go faster? Is this guy crazy or what? No, Dr. Phil Maffetone is not crazy, and I feel very fortunate to have met him when I did. I have been a professional triathlete since 1984. When I started my career, I just picked up the triathlon magazine to see what the top pros were doing and then just tried to emulate them. The one guy who was a star at the time was Scott Molina. He was doing mega miles in all three sports, plus doing speed workouts for each of the disciplines — swimming, cycling and running. It looked like a good way to be the best, especially if you had the time to just eat, sleep, swim, bike and run. Things went well for me during the first three years. In 1988, I was able to work my way up to the top rank. I thought I was invincible. That is when the road began to get bumpy. Suddenly I had no control over my progression. I was also starting to lose my love for the sport. It got so bad that I was about to quit and move on. The training became too hard and the results weren't there to justify the pain. That's about the time I met Phil.

We sat down and had a long talk. At first it was hard for me to swallow what Phil had to say. What helped me is that I have spent a lot of time training with Mark Allen. What I knew from training with Mark was that his heart rate was always 10 to 15 beats lower than mine during long rides. During our long rides the pace would be even the first 65 miles then I would start to die a slow death out on the plains near Boulder, Colorado. I was like the hummingbird who needed fuel all the time, and Mark was like a steam engine that you feed coal and it cruises for hours and hours.

Also, I was impressed by how consistent Mark's career was going with very few flaws year after year. But the topper of it all was that Mark had already been following Phil's plan for many years.

So I listened to Phil with both ears wide open. After our conversation, Phil gave me one of his books. It was an easy-reading book that offered a lot of common sense about how to train and eat properly. So, I decided to follow his "180 Formula" for determining aerobic heart rate, and over a little time I have become a firm believer in this training program.

At first the training seemed slow at my designated heart rate of 155. There were times when I had to walk up hills during the run and zig-zag on the bike just to stay in my aerobic range. But with time, things started to change and I became stronger at the same heart rate. This was quite exciting. After five months of loyal training, I got my first big sign that the program was working.

Before going on the program, I would ride to my parents' summer place which is 65 miles with three good climbs. My previous record was set with a good friend of mine. We had the total grudge match all the way to find who was king of the bike. He would attack on the hills and I was holding a heart rate between 165 and 182 to establish a "record" of 3 hours and 15 minutes. When we arrived at the cabin I achieved a total bonk. The best I could do for the rest of the day was eat and sleep — and even that was difficult. Three years later after five months on Phil's aerobic program, I attempted the same course again. This time I rode solo and never went above 155 even on the long climb. The results were astounding. I went 3:09 and felt good enough to go for a 10-mile run straight after. Now I was convinced that the program was working.

The next test was the first race of the season while following Phil's plan. It is amazing how I was seeing good aerobic results in my workouts but still had doubts about my performance level. You see, I still needed my hammer sessions to prove to me or build my confidence that I was ready to race at a professional level. The season opener was in Australia at Surfer's Paradise International Triathlon. My confidence was so blown that I didn't even want to get on the plane. But a swift kick from my wife and I was off. The whole week prior to the race I was fighting myself, saying that I wasn't going to do well because of a lack of speed training. Finally, I told myself to shut up and go have a good time. To my surprise

I did have a good time — and won! The speed was there and my endurance was definitely there, too. But the biggest bonus was that I was able to beat Mark Allen at his own game.

Now I am hooked. I am in love with my profession and I am staying healthy at the same time. Dr. Maffetone's guidelines are easy. All you need is a heart-rate monitor to listen to your ticker and a little patience. And yes, you can do it just by slowing down and letting your body catch up with your mind.

Best wishes,

— Mike Pigg

Introduction

My athletic career started in 1968 when I answered an ad in the local paper announcing swim-team tryouts. At the time I literally couldn't swim more than the length of a 25-yard pool without having to stop and catch my breath. In the nearly 30 years since, I have tried almost every training theory and coaching style in the pursuit of my personal athletic excellence. The evolution to my present program was not easy. The years of regimented swim coaching had ingrained in me a very narrow-minded training philosophy, which was to do more faster. If I could just train more yardage, and train faster, then I would most certainly race faster. Or so I thought.

My race results from this type of program were mediocre at best. Do more faster really only works for those so talented that their genetics override the lunacy of their training and take them to greatness anyway. I ended my 12-year swimming career completely burned out physically and mentally. I also ended it feeling like I just didn't reach my potential. But at the time, I couldn't put my finger on the answer as to why.

Fortunately, I was given a second chance to explore the limits of my athletic abilities. In 1982 I embarked on what has been a dream trip through the world of triathlon. It wasn't always smooth, though. My initiation years were a mirror to my swimming career. A few great results were separated by injuries and sporadic improvement, due specifically to the swimming mentality of do more faster. But unlike swimming, which is not an impact sport, the price of unwise training in triathlons is not only mental decay, but physical as well. Something needed to change.

Just about this time I was introduced to Dr. Phil Maffetone, who had enjoyed a good deal of success training some local triathletes. I was warned that his methods were probably going to sound crazy at first, but that they really worked. That was 1984. And yes, at the time his philosophy on training was almost completely opposite from my do more faster approach. Now it's a new millennium, and his training techniques which once seemed crazy are almost universally accepted as the only method that will allow you to reach your peak performance year after year. Using Phil's training program and consulting with him over the years, I have been able to rack up a long list of international triathlon victories, including six Hawaiian Ironman titles, the last of which came at age 37!

In the pages that follow, Dr. Maffetone details the training philosophy that I have used throughout my triathlon career. If you have used these tools, you know they work. If you haven't, welcome to what will undoubtedly be a whole new level of athletic performance. Take the time to follow his program. Leave your ego at the door, because in the short term it might seem like you aren't going anywhere. But long term, I guarantee you will see the results you know your body is capable of.

See you at the races,

> — *Mark Allen, six-time Hawaii Ironman champion*
> *and world record holder*

1

The Art and Science of Endurance

It was without conscious design that becoming a coach (a word I'll use synonymously with trainer) became part of my professional career. My diverse athletic background included many coaches, most of whom trained me no differently than the rest of the team. I recognized years ago that most coaching was done in this "cookbook" fashion, with no individual considerations.

Once I entered private practice it became evident that coaching had to be part of caring for athletes. I was an applied kinesiologist with a good understanding of the true sense of the word "holistic." And treating an athlete also meant extending that care into his or her lifestyle.

The most important aspect of this "total athlete" concept was assessment — getting feedback from the athlete about how the body was functioning. This includes not only conscious reactions of how the person was feeling, but also more objective, measurable data which would assist both of us in developing an ideal training program from month to month, and from year to year.

After beginning private practice in 1977, I quickly learned an important lesson in caring for the athletic patient. A local runner, Andy, came to see me with a leg injury. The problem seemed simple to correct, and he was out of pain after his second visit. But a month later, he returned with a similar symptom. I treated him again, and obtained equally good results. But several weeks later Andy returned with a different injury, a problem in the low back.

Although I evaluated Andy's diet and asked about other potential stress, one mistake I made was presuming he knew how to train. Although he understood the basics, he could not individualize his training to meet his particular needs. That is a difficult task for anyone to do properly.

Before I realized it was time to take a closer look at his training, Andy was gone. He sought relief from another doctor. Unfortunately, his journey from one professional to another continued for some time, as it had before me. While I lost track of his travels, he taught me a great lesson, one I previously could only conceptualize: Look at the big picture.

After my experience with Andy, I looked at every athlete's diary, and had them tell me in detail how they were training and competing. I realized that part of my treatment, if I were to take a holistic view, had to include modifying the athlete's training schedule, if necessary, to make it fit with everything else in his or her life.

For the endurance athlete, that is what I would like to share in this book — a view of the whole story, the big picture. Every aspect of your life affects all others. And if you want to succeed in your training and competition, a wide-angle view is the best approach.

This is a book about my program for the endurance athlete. It combines experiences and observations, academic facts and theories of mine and others from many fields of health care and sports. The main focus is outcome: what works best for an individual athlete at a given point in his or her life. It is a program that combines both the art and science of training and racing.

But there are some ground rules that must be followed. They are not my rules, but nature's. The first and most important is that what is done in training and racing be health-promoting. In other words, it's not acceptable to sacrifice your health to be a better athlete. If you do, you'll pay the penalty in the form of injury or ill health somewhere down the road. This idea was obvious early in my career, and I set forth some basic definitions of health and fitness. I'll repeat them here because they are so important.

Health is a state where all the body's systems are working in harmony. These include not just the muscular system, but the circulatory, skeletal, hormonal, lymphatic, nervous systems and all other parts of the body.

Fitness is the ability to be athletic. The more fit a person has become, the more effective he or she will compete.

Injuries, sickness, fatigue and other symptoms common to many athletes are indications of an imbalance between health and fitness. While these problems are common, they are not normal in endurance sports like they are in contact events. It is unfortunate that most athletes are willing, consciously or not, to sacrifice health for more fitness.

While my program was developed for the typical endurance athlete, it assumes everyone is unique, with specific needs. Whether you are a seasoned professional or a beginner, this program will work because you will be able to tailor it to fit your many individual needs.

The case histories in this book are real, with the names changed. They serve as real-life examples, and demonstrate that your problems are often shared by many other endurance athletes. And more importantly, correction of these problems, along with prevention, is quite often easily managed.

As humans, we are all endurance athletes. Those of us who choose to develop our natural talents more fully in order to compete must rely on training proficiency. But why can't we depend on intuition? I believe our instincts hold great powers. But in allowing that sense to be useful, it must maneuver through your conscious mind. Here is where potential problems may exist. We have all grown up with many influences, including positive and negative ones. Some have become our beliefs in the form of tradition. These attitudes, such as "no pain, no gain" are well ingrained in our brains. Others are more subtly deposited, the result of media hype and advertising propaganda. These life-long recordings can easily cloud natural instinct, making intuitive training very difficult. In time, however, by learning more about your body and its needs, training and racing by intuition can be your most effective technique. This is the method we should all strive to achieve. Ultimately, that is what this book is about.

2

Definitions for Modern Athletes

A sk a dozen seasoned endurance athletes what the word endurance means, and you're likely to get a dozen different definitions. In endurance circles, common everyday words can have a variety of meanings, sometimes with dramatic differences.

Part of the problem of defining endurance stems from the fact that this word has many different meanings for many different people. As a common term, *Funk & Wagnall's New International Dictionary* defines endurance as "the capacity or power to endure; ability to suffer pain, distress, hardship, or any very prolonged stress without succumbing; patient fortitude." But the 25th edition of *Dorland's Medical Dictionary* doesn't even list the word.

Even in academic circles, definitions can vary. In *Exercise Physiology*, McArdle defines endurance as "the time limit of a person's ability to maintain either a specific isometric force or a specific power level involving combination of concentric or eccentric muscular contractions." And in *Physiology of Sport and Exercise*, Wilmore and Costill describe it as "the ability to resist fatigue; includes muscular endurance and cardiorespiratory endurance." While these are important academic explanations, few endurance athletes and coaches can relate to them in practical, useful ways.

Without a common definition of endurance we all can relate to, interpreting the information in this book may be difficult. So allow me to propose a definition useful for the endurance field, one we can all relate to more in training and racing than in a laboratory.

My definition for endurance relates to athletes who engage in training for durations of more than about 5 to 10 minutes:

- A steady-state level of activity where one can develop and sustain relatively high speeds at submaximum effort over time.

- The ability to develop higher speeds while remaining predominantly aerobic.

- Increasing the percent fat-burning and decreasing the dependence on carbohydrate utilization with training.

An important aspect of endurance is that it should not only persist for many years, but improve annually; with a peak not being reached until the latter part of the third or well into the fourth decade of life.

Obviously, I don't include track and field sprinters in this category of endurance athletes. However, they have some similar needs and may benefit greatly by following many of the techniques and philosophies described in this book.

Some humans possess great sprinting ability. By sprinting, I refer to the very short activity which lasts from only a few seconds up to less than a minute. One unique difference between sprinters and endurance athletes is genetics. Bouchard and his colleagues at Laval University in Quebec City have shown in research what many coaches have known for years — that sprinters are born and endurance athletes are made. He concluded that the anaerobic power found in world-class sprinters like Carl Lewis is 92 percent inherited, while endurance champions like six-time Hawaii Ironman Triathlon champion Mark Allen inherit only 25 percent of their ability, with the remainder coming through training.

Endurance athletes include triathletes and duathletes, runners, cyclists, mountain bikers, swimmers, skaters and cross-country skiers. But others not usually thought of as endurance athletes must possess endurance ability or they will succumb to injury and short athletic lifespans. These include basketball, hockey, football, soccer and baseball players, and even race-car drivers.

Endurance sports, in both natural and organized forms, have existed for centuries. But as an established class, today's endurance athletes, who by far outnumber athletes who participate in sprint events, have been influenced more by the philosophies used to train sprinters than by distance coaches, athletes and others.

Case History

Larry was a great sprinter in high school and college, performing well at 100 and 200 meters, the long jump and short indoor distances. Now at 37, and an endurance athlete, Larry's training program still included track workouts from spring through early winter. On the track he would perform sprint drills, do 200-, 400- and 800-meter repeats and occasionally a 5K time trial. But Larry was often injured and his 5K time trials were often better than his races for the same distance. When I began working with Larry, he had a difficult time with a schedule that did not include sprint workouts. But he was delighted with the results, which included being injury free and achieving personal bests. He finally realized that performing on the roads was really a different sport than what he did in his early track days.

As the running, cycling and triathlon boom evolved, influential personalities, especially coaches and well-known athletes from track and field and other sprint sports, including swimming and biking, emerged too. As a result of their presence and their training techniques, the trend of training like a sprinter was maintained. As a result, today's endurance athletes often hold on to that tradition of sprint workouts — track, road or pool intervals — to increase speed.

If you look at the time commitment associated with these anaerobic benefits, and weigh them against the benefits in competition, you'll get a better picture. For example, in a one-hour event, only 2 percent of your energy is derived from the anaerobic system. In a two-hour event, only 1 percent of your energy is derived from anaerobic sources. Does it make sense to spend so many hours a week on anaerobic work when 99 percent of your race is aerobic?

As I will discuss in detail in later chapters, you should derive most of your endurance speed from aerobic training. But before moving on to these other topics, more definitions are necessary. Two important ones are the terms aerobic and anaerobic.

Take a snapshot of the body's metabolism, and the most obvious feature is oxygen. As everyone knows, oxygen is essential for energy production. But not all energy is obtained with the help of oxygen. We can get energy from reactions that require oxygen, and energy that does not need oxygen. When oxygen is used to generate energy, it is called aerobic, and when the body derives energy without using oxygen it is termed anaerobic. This is the common way athletes and coaches look at these definitions.

However, this scheme refers to the conversion of sugar or glucose. In reality, sugar (originating mostly from dietary carbohydrates) is only one of two main sources of energy. The other is fat.

Depending on a person's training and nutrition, and state of health, as much as 80 to 90 percent of total energy can be derived from fat. The conversion of fat to energy takes place in the slow-twitch or red muscle fibers. These are also referred to as aerobic muscle fibers. These muscle fibers are used during longer, relatively slower activity. When an endurance athlete fatigues in a race, it is associated with the loss of available glucose necessary to sustain the conversion of fat to energy in the aerobic muscle fiber.

The specific muscle fiber where glucose is converted to energy is the fast-twitch or white muscle fiber, also referred to as the anaerobic muscle fiber. These muscle fibers are used for short-distance speed, since anaerobic energy is limited to 1 to 3 minutes.

Classic definitions of "aerobic" and "anaerobic" relate to either the need for oxygen, or its absence. But they often do not take into account the source of the energy — sugar or fat — which is a distinguishing feature, or the muscle fibers which not only convert sugar or fat to energy, but propel the athlete during training and racing.

I propose a definition of aerobic and anaerobic based on both the source of energy and the type of muscle fiber used. Relating aerobic and anaerobic this way to training and racing makes it a more simple, complete and useful definition.

Aerobic: The ability of the body to use more fats and less sugar (glucose) for energy.

Anaerobic: The ability of the body to use more
sugar (glucose) and less fat for energy.

While we separate specific aspects of the body in the ways described above for convenience, the truth is all components of the body work together in harmony. For example, we nearly always use both glucose and fat for energy, and both aerobic and anaerobic muscle fibers are used during endurance activity.

We see this harmony best when measuring the amount of glucose and fat the body is using at a given intensity during training. The respiratory quotient (RQ) or respiratory exchange ratio (RER) is the amount of carbon dioxide exhaled divided by the oxygen consumed. From this number it is possible to obtain a fairly accurate percentage of glucose and fat used for energy. For example, a ratio of .85 indicates that about half the energy used is derived from glucose, and half from fats.

As endurance improves, so does the use of fats for energy. This fat-burning may increase to 50, 60 or 70 percent or more at submaximum intensities. In disciplined athletes tremendous values for fat-burning have been obtained. The following chart was compiled on triathlete Mike Pigg:

Heart Rate	RQ	%Fat	%Sugar
127	.79	70	30
133	.80	67	33
135	.82	60	40
137	.83	56	44
141	.84	53	47
146	.82	60	40
153	.85	50	50
153	.85	50	50
155*	.87	42	58
164	.87	42	58
169	.90	32	68

*At 155 heart rate, Mike can run sub-5:25 pace.

This brief introduction to aerobic and anaerobic metabolism is only the tip of a very large and complex iceberg. My definition of aerobic and anaerobic has been simplified and made more useful for endurance athletes and not necessarily for the professional doing laboratory research. More importantly, it is a practical way to relate to training and racing, as we shall see.

Even more useful are some simple definitions of the word "training." Although this explanation is in the form of an equation, it is very important to always remember it:

Training = Work + Rest

More specifically, work is your workout; the daily training routine which builds muscles, improves their efficiency, increases oxygen uptake, etc. In physiology it's called overload. In the case of a muscle, you must work it slightly harder than it is used to in order to rebuild and improve its function.

But work is not limited to your training. It can also mean house, yard or office work, taking care of the kids, shopping, etc. This activity still burns fat and sugar, works the muscles, stimulates the metabolism and nervous system. Although it won't necessarily help you in training, it must be considered because it is still work and it requires recovery.

An important part of the equation is rest. It is during this rest phase that your body recovers from training. It allows your muscles and other working parts to rebuild and prepare for the next bout of training. During this phase, there should be no training, and sufficient sleep. But if you have to work, shop or take care of the kids, you're not resting as much as you can. Since most athletes don't have the luxury of complete rest, care must be taken to avoid training beyond one's ability to recover from it. For most, that means cut down on training to keep the equation balanced.

If you don't provide enough rest, your body will not be ready for more work. Or, if you work beyond the muscle's or body's ability to rest or recover from the workload, you overtrain. Any of these imbalances can result in a series of malfunctions which may cause injury, ill health or burnout. An imbalanced training equation leads to overtraining, as discussed in detail in a later chapter.

For most athletes the work part of the equation is actually the easy aspect of training. It is the rest phase that is most often neglected.

Case History

Bob was a good local runner who desperately wanted to improve. But his expanding business and growing family was demanding more time from his busy training schedule. He tried to accommodate everyone and maintain his training. He woke up early every morning to get in his daily run. Within a few months he was exhausted and began feeling pain in his knees and back. In the middle of a very successful racing season, his times began to deteriorate. The first thing I recommended when Bob consulted me was to cut his training down by about 40 percent, since he was not able to decrease any of his other commitments. Almost immediately his energy improved and his physical problems disappeared. After about four weeks on his modified schedule, Bob ran a great race, and continued racing well for the rest of the season.

If you work a full-time job, have a family, a house or all of the above, you're busy. You can still work out and train successfully if you balance the equation. Of all the endurance athletes I initially saw when I was in practice, most were working out far more than necessary. In my years of training athletes, I have spent a good deal of time convincing athletes to cut down. When they do, they feel better, work out more efficiently and their performance improves.

Definitions should be useful for those who are involved in the process. Keeping the definitions of endurance, training, aerobic and anaerobic both simple and practical helps everyone understand the bigger picture.

3

The Practical Science of Training

No one really knows everything about endurance training. While science has come a long way, we still understand only a small piece of the big puzzle. But we are not lost between the hypothetical ideals of the perfect intuitive athlete and the flawlessly engineered scientific specimen. There can be logic in training, along with intuition. It is here that both art and science come together.

In this chapter, I would like to explore the scientific aspect of training, specifically the mechanisms influenced when you train, and how training in turn affects your body. It is these mechanisms which give back what you ask for in health and performance.

When viewing the science of training, understand that all that is known is not black and white. Scientists continually debate many aspects of this field, and just as many attitudes, theories and facts are changed over time due to new research and observations. My point here is that science as we know it is not an exact science. And, the view you get here is mine. My academic background is very extensive, and much of my day is spent in textbooks and journal articles. But if the scientific aspect of training presented here is not relative, interesting and simplified, you will soon be asleep.

The attempt is to make compatible the science and the clinical observations made in the athletes I work with. In many ways, they are my experiments. Through the trial-and-error process, we all learn how to succeed in sports, and how to build a healthier body and mind.

23

In a sense, there are several bodies within you, each representing different aspects of your physiology. When you train, these different parts are programmed to work in a very specific way. But what you ask your body to learn in training is not always what you really want it to do. An example of this is the development of speed. Old wisdom tells you that if you want to race fast, you must train fast. In one sense that seems logical. But in endurance sports what you get from training fast like a sprinter is not acceptable. The result is you will obtain speed meant for a sprinter — short-term and short-lived. If you try to apply this type of training to endurance activity, you run the risk of overtraining. While we all have an obsession for speed, this does not fit the definition of, or the desire for, endurance. The different bodies within you which must be trained for endurance include the muscles, metabolism and the nerves.

Your workout trains the muscles, which are obviously vital in any athletic action. But they react only when, and how the nervous system tells them to do so. That same workout also influences the nerves that attach to the muscles, while at the same time other parts of the nervous system affect the metabolism. Your energy is provided for by the metabolism so the muscles can perform. Each aspect of the body is in constant interaction with all the others, and what you do in training has significant influence over the whole body.

Let's take a closer look at these aspects of the body, the nervous system, the metabolism and the muscles, and see how each is intricately related to training.

Training the Nervous System

Perhaps the most important part of your body, the one most responsive to training and most important for competition, is the nervous system. All physiological activity is influenced by this system. In many ways, when we talk about training, we're referring to the neurological mechanisms.

Picture a large house with hundreds of meters of wires, some very thin, some large cables, all connecting together and controlled from a central switch box. The nervous system runs through your body in a similar way. Except it goes to every square millimeter of the body, and sends information both ways. The main processing center of the nervous system is the brain and spinal cord housed within your spine.

A good illustration of the nervous system's interrelationships throughout the body is its connection to the muscles — referred to as the neuromuscular junction. Each aerobic muscle fiber has a separate nerve connecting to it. The same is true with the anaerobic fibers. And that type of nerve fiber has a specific action much like the muscle fiber itself. For example, the nerve fiber attaching to the slow-twitch aerobic fiber is slower acting compared to the nerve fiber which joins the fast-twitch anaerobic muscle fiber, which is faster-acting.

Training the slower nerves to stimulate their specific aerobic fibers — which work at submaximal efforts — is one key to building successful endurance. But this does not mean you will always be "slow" — the biggest fear all athletes have. In time, and with successful training, the slow-twitch aerobic muscles improve function and increase their speed, but still function as a slow-twitch fiber.

If you don't train these specific parts of the nervous system, along with their connections with the aerobic muscles, and as many as possible, you'll never "learn" to build high-quality aerobic activity. In training circles this is called building an aerobic base. In neurological terms, it is referred to as an engram. Engrams are stored memories in the brain.

One unique ability of the nervous system is its capacity to learn. We've all experienced it. Learning how to type, play the piano or perform any skill you learn by practice is the result of implanting memory into the nervous system. In the same way, training for endurance is no different. Each workout is a small part of a memory stored in the brain.

If you train indiscriminately, that is stored as a permanent record in your nervous system. If you overtrain, that too is registered. But if you train effectively, you maintain that memory too. The nervous system remembers everything it experiences, so be careful what you put into it. Sometimes a long process of "re-training" is necessary, especially in those who have abused their bodies through improper training.

You can train your nervous system to function efficiently at a high endurance level. In order to do that, you have to influence the nerves that attach to the aerobic muscles. But you have to stimulate all of them, beginning with the smallest aerobic fibers, which move you very slowly. Over time, as these nerves and muscles are trained, they work more efficiently. The result is they can do more work with the same effort. This translates into more speed from muscles and nerves that once were much slower.

The importance of the nervous system is exemplified in its influence on the muscle's power. Everyone thinks that the anaerobic muscles are more powerful in their actions than the slower-moving aerobic ones. But this is untrue. Aerobic and anaerobic muscle fibers can generate the same potential force. The difference between them is neurological. When the nervous system calls for anaerobic action, more muscle fibers are activated into action by nerves compared to the same stimulation of aerobic muscles.

Training the Muscles

For most endurance athletes, too much focus in training is on the muscles. If they were the primary element in endurance, then weight-lifting would provide more success than any other training technique. But the muscles are just pawns in the endurance game. They are the work horses. And if we drive them too hard or not enough, we get less performance. However, the muscles still play an important role in endurance.

The aerobic muscle fibers are uniquely different from their anaerobic counterparts. Aerobic fibers are sometimes called "red" because they contain structures called mitochondria which contain the iron-protein, red-pigmented compound myoglobin. It is here, through myoglobin action in the mitochondria, that oxygen is successfully used in the energy-generating process. The more these muscle fibers are trained, the more mitochondria and myoglobin is created, and the more oxygen will be utilized to help produce energy. The mitochondria is also the site of fat-burning.

Also unique to the aerobic muscle fiber is that it is generally fatigue-resistant. Over time, aerobic fatigue is due to the nervous and metabolic aspects as discussed below. Even after 10 hours of racing, there is still unused glycogen in the anaerobic fibers — unless you used it inadvertently during the event. If this small reserve is still intact, it is quite useful for your final kick.

Another important characteristic of the aerobic fiber is its high concentration of blood vessels. Arteries bring blood into the fiber, along with oxygen and nutrients, including vitamins, minerals and fats. The veins bring blood out, carrying by-products such as carbon dioxide and lactic acid. These substances must be removed as quickly as possible since they have the potential to slow the muscle's action.

Through endurance training you should develop much more circulation than would normally be possible. When aerobic fibers are left untrained, their potential blood vessels are also left unused. Transport of oxygen to the muscles is one of the limiting factors in performance.

Training all the aerobic muscle fibers allows the use of the full spectrum of muscle — from the smallest walking fibers to the relatively fast aerobic ones. By doing that, you increase circulation, improve oxygen utilization, burn more fat, remove more by-products and function more efficiently.

The aerobic fibers are the most commonly contracted part of the muscle, even in everyday action. Your physical activity at work and home, shopping and doing everyday chores requires aerobic muscle activity. This is where the potential risk of overtraining is of concern, not from your workout but from all other activity you do in the course of the normal day or week. The sum of all your activity must be balanced if you are to get maximum training benefits and avoid overtraining.

Endurance training should involve the use of as many aerobic fibers as possible. In doing so, we can't help using some of the anaerobic fibers. But the predominance will be in training the aerobic muscles. Even walking, which activates the very-slow-moving aerobic fibers, has a place in endurance training, especially for the professional athlete.

The anaerobic muscles are our sprinting, power fibers, and are generally much larger than the aerobic ones. The anaerobic fibers are actually made up of three different kinds. The scientific terminology varies dramatically, but I will simply refer to the anaerobic fibers as a, b and c types.

The type "a" fibers are really a combination of aerobic and anaerobic quality. These fibers are very important in endurance training and racing. When these fibers are highly developed, they are much like an aerobic fiber. Developing their aerobic quality further improves endurance, and most especially what I call "aerobic speed."

Building aerobic speed means developing the ability to go faster with the same or less effort. For example a runner who runs 5,000 meters in 18 minutes at a determined heart rate may in a short time improve to run that same distance in 17 minutes or even faster at the same heart rate. The concept is applicable to all sports — distance cyclists, swimmers, or cross-country skiers can all program their bodies to go faster with the same or less energy, and for longer periods of time.

The type "b" fibers are the pure anaerobic types. They are made for power and short bursts of speed, but can only function for a very brief period of time — perhaps 2 to 3 minutes or less. These fibers rely exclusively on sugar for energy. The main reason their function is so short-term is because both glucose and glycogen are very limited.

Not nearly as much is known about the type "c" anaerobic fibers. These are found only in small numbers within the anaerobic population of fibers.

All muscles in the human body contain all the fibers mentioned above. They are assembled side by side in a seemingly random order. The different fibers are used when required. For example, during walking almost all the muscle action is from aerobic fibers. If you walk faster, more aerobic muscle is enlisted. Begin to jog and the "a" type anaerobic fibers are added into action, and as you increase your speed to higher intensity, more "b" type anaerobic fibers take over. But with faster activity the slower-moving aerobic fibers reduce their action.

In some animals, like a chicken, different muscles have more exclusive fiber types. For example, the chicken's legs contain mostly aerobic muscle fibers; they are used for slow, constant walking. The "breast," however, is composed of mostly anaerobic fibers — the white meat — used for fast, powerful, short-lived flapping of the wings.

The percentage of different fibers in a given muscle varies between people. Certain muscles of elite endurance athletes contain up to 90 percent aerobic fibers, where sprinters may have as little as 25 percent, with the remainder being anaerobic. But remember that the anaerobic type "a" has significant aerobic function, so simply counting aerobic and anaerobic fibers can be misleading when relating to overall function. It is my opinion that some of the great sprinters can be trained to make great endurance athletes.

Knowing the percentage of aerobic and anaerobic muscle fibers, however, will do little in ascertaining that person's performance outcome. This is because the muscle itself is not the determining factor in performance, but the sum of the neurological, muscular and metabolic activity and efficiency.

In endurance athletes, the training effect more than makes up for any individual difference in fiber type and genetics. While your particular fiber make-up is mostly genetically determined, your training determines the efficiency of those fibers. Also, some interesting changes may occur in training.

Can aerobic fibers be trained to change to anaerobic fibers, or vice versa? There is considerable controversy over whether fiber types can switch as a result of training. My personal opinion is they can.

Studies show that anaerobic training decreases the number of aerobic fibers and increases the number of type "c" anaerobic fibers. With aerobic training, there is an increase in the number of aerobic fibers. Another study showed similar results: a 23 percent increase in anaerobic fibers and the same percent decrease in aerobic fibers with only six weeks of sprint training. Inactivity, or detraining, may also decrease aerobic fiber percentages.

In addition, with age you lose some of your anaerobic fibers which results in a higher percentage of aerobic fibers in each muscle. This is one main reason why sprinters reach their peak early in life, and endurance athletes don't peak until the third or fourth decade, and can still continue to perform at high levels for many years beyond that time.

As we all have experienced, muscles ultimately fatigue in the course of endurance activity. But it is not the muscle itself which tires. It's usually a combination of the neurological aspects we discussed above and the metabolic factors addressed below.

Over time in training or racing, there is a slowing and finally a cessation of nerve transmission to the muscle. The reasons for this are unknown. Metabolically, the muscle can run out of fuel (sugar and fat) even if enough oxygen and neurological stimulation is present. (In short sprints, fatigue occurs from a lack of oxygen.) This is usually the result of using up too much sugar by training or racing too hard.

Metabolic Training

Endurance training and competition requires moderate amounts of energy over long periods of time. This is different from sprinters who use very large amounts of energy in a very short time period. But the energy used for every action has a long journey before we can access it.

All energy used for training and racing originates as light energy from the sun. Plants take in this energy, convert it and store it as chemical energy. We consume the plants or eat animals who feed on plants. The energy is transferred to us in the form of carbohydrates, proteins and fats, and we use it as mechanical energy.

Converting the foods you eat into usable energy for muscle action is the job of your metabolism. The quality of the food eaten and the efficiency of metabolism helps produce energy for training and performance.

Carbohydrates, proteins and fats are eaten and chemically broken down in the intestine and absorbed as glucose, amino acids and small fat particles. These food products are gradually separated into smaller chemicals. Eventually, on a molecular level, adenosine triphosphate (ATP) is produced. The ATP from food is used as energy for all biological work.

Three methods of harnessing energy exist in your body. They are referred to as the creatine phosphate (CP), anaerobic and aerobic systems.

The CP system is the most immediate energy source. The energy produced in this system is very limited. For example, at the beginning of a 100-meter sprint, an athlete may use CP for some of his or her energy. The CP system only has about 5 to 10 seconds worth of energy. This system will only be mentioned here, because it is emphasized less and its benefits minimized in endurance training relative to the other two systems.

For energy to be maintained beyond the time limits of creatine phosphate, the anaerobic system is utilized. Energy from this system is derived from glucose in the anaerobic muscle fiber. Ideally, this energy system is most useful at the end of endurance competition, where a final kick is needed. But the maximum amount of energy the anaerobic system can generate is about 3 minutes worth of all-out effort. If you use up this energy too early in competition, you can adversely and sometimes tragically affect overall performance.

As we all know, a unique feature of the anaerobic system is that the process of energy production also generates lactic acid. As we mentioned earlier, there is always some anaerobic muscle activity, so there is a constant production of lactic acid in the anaerobic muscle. At rest and during submaximal activity, the small amount of lactic acid produced is eliminated quickly. It is only at high intensities that it accumulates. (Lactic acid is transported to the blood where it is chemically changed and called blood lactate.) In part, this accumulation of lactic acid restricts your performance.

With intense training and competition, most endurance athletes race with levels of blood lactate that are much higher than resting, often significantly. Actually, race pace is limited to a great extent by the accumulation of blood lactate. This increase in lactic acid can be controlled best if the body has substantial development of aerobic muscle fiber. In general, the better your aerobic base, the less lactate is produced. Removal of lactic acid is also more efficient when the blood circulation is more developed, which coincides with improvement in aerobic muscle fiber. Even neighboring aerobic muscle fibers which are inactive during more intense activity are capable of eliminating or oxidizing lactic acid.

The blood lactate level may be a very accurate predictor of performance and a successful way to monitor training quality. Studies using endurance athletes show that the race times were highly correlated with blood lactate. Evaluating maximum oxygen uptake (VO_2 max) is not only a poor predictor of actual performance, but an ineffective indicator of training efficiency.

In general, blood-lactate levels return to normal resting levels within about 20 minutes after training or racing. The feeling of muscle soreness following activity is most likely due to the normal wear and tear on the muscle fibers.

Since the body has strict limitations on energy gained from the anaerobic system, a third source of energy, and the main focus for endurance training, is available.

The most important long-term energy source comes from the aerobic system. Its characteristic feature is that significant amounts of energy can be derived from the conversion of fat in the aerobic muscle fiber. The aerobic system, with its use of fat, has up to 75,000 kcal of energy available — enough abundant energy reserve to maintain training or racing for many hours, or even days.

Triglycerides are the main fats used for energy. When chemically broken down in fat stores they enter the bloodstream as free fatty acids (FFA), where they are carried to the aerobic muscles and burned in the mitochondria for energy. This process of burning fat is called beta oxidation.

In addition to burning fat, the aerobic system also uses some glucose for energy production. Even in the breakdown of triglycerides to FFA, glycerine which is normally stored in the fat molecule is released, converted to glucose and used for energy.

The utilization of glucose by the aerobic system is vital because it maintains the fat-burning process. During training or racing, if you deplete your glucose and glycogen stores, fat-burning will also cease.

Herein lies the endurance game; as the time of your activity increases, more fat and aerobic energy must be generated. But as the intensity increases, less oxygen is delivered, so aerobic metabolism is diminished, forcing the body to use more anaerobic energy, which is much more limited. If you use up all your glucose, even fat-burning stops, along with the rest of your body. Do you refrain from going faster so you can go farther? Can you really go farther and faster?

You can have the best of both; the answer is in your training. By properly programming your body, you can develop both endurance and aerobic speed, the focus of later chapters. This program is based on time and intensity, rather than miles and pace.

Another way of explaining this program is that you are able to burn a higher percentage of fat — and lower amounts of sugar — at higher levels of intensity.

If you are not yet encouraged to focus more on aerobic instead of anaerobic training, here is another important factor. The percentage of aerobic and anaerobic activity in workouts or races of different duration is an important consideration. The table below indicates how much aerobic and anaerobic energy is used during maximal activity.

This is an extremely brief view of the body's metabolism. The chemical activity which takes place in the body every moment during training

Time (Minutes)	Percent Anaerobic	Percent Aerobic
1	70	30
2	50	50
4	35	65
10	15	85
30	5	95
60	2	98
120	1	99
>120	<1	>99

and racing, and at rest, is very complex. For example, there are at least 900 enzymes known to be involved with metabolism. Just the breakdown of sugar to energy requires 19 different chemical reactions. And it's not just the metabolism that is complex, but all the systems of the body and how they interrelate.

Let me offer one final note about our discussion on the different aspects of the body — neurological, muscular and metabolic — and their role in training. It has been my observation that each aspect of the body progresses at slightly different rates.

You may perceive this in different ways. Your perceived exertion at the same intensity may not always feel the same. For example, when athletes first start on my program, the biggest complaint is they don't feel they are getting much of a workout because of the relatively slow pace. During that phase, the muscles are more developed than the aerobic metabolism. But in time, this situation changes.

By developing your aerobic metabolism you are eventually able to train at a faster rate with less effort. You may then have more physical difficulty because your muscular and neurological body has not kept pace with the progressing aerobic metabolism. Athletes may then complain that, despite a low training heart rate, they have to work very hard.

Training is much like conducting a symphony; there are many players which must be working in precise harmony to produce a great performance. We have talked about three main parts of the body and their effects on and from training. But as you can see, each part has many smaller pieces that are vital to the success of the whole.

4

The MAF Program

The information in this book provides the basic tools necessary to improve not only your endurance, but also your health. As your aerobic system develops and endurance improves, you'll notice your speed also increases at the same level of exertion, i.e., heart rate. This will in turn make for better competitive performances. This improvement should continue for years and even decades.

Continued aerobic improvement is assessed with objective self-evaluations made throughout the year. This monitoring is necessary in order to fine tune your training and avoid the potential dangers. Effective evaluation is accomplished by understanding some simple techniques and using a heart-rate monitor as a biofeedback tool.

Dorland's Medical Dictionary defines biofeedback as "the process of providing visual or auditory evidence to a person of the status of body function so that you may exert control over that function."

As a student involved in a biofeedback research project, I measured responses in human subjects to various physiological inputs, such as sounds, visual effects and various physical stimulation, including exercise. The observed reactions were evaluated by measuring temperature, perspiration and heart rate. Through this research, it became evident that using the heart rate to objectively measure body function was simple, accurate and useful. And its application in sports was obvious.

There are three important applications of heart-rate monitoring for endurance athletes:

- Training

- Assessment

- Competition

Essentially, what is being measured is the maximum aerobic function — MAF — of the athlete. MAF can be measured during any endurance activity such as swimming, biking or running. The MAF is the foundation of endurance efficiency, and the source of aerobic speed, stamina and long-term improvements in performance. Even anaerobic benefits will result from developing maximum aerobic function.

Before discussing the specifics of training, assessment and competition, I would like to give you the historical perspective of how this program was developed.

In my early years in practice in the late 1970s, I began using the large, bulky heart-rate monitoring units available then to monitor the training of an increasing number of athletes. It was a tool to assess the quality of these athletes' workouts, and allowed me to assess whether an athlete was working too hard for the prescribed training, or perhaps not strenuously enough.

Before heart monitors were available, pulse rates were determined manually, and athletes would take their own pulses. But I found their accuracy was generally not good when compared to ECG readings. Manual pulses usually arrived at heart rates too low compared to the actual rate determined by pulse meters. When I took the athlete's pulse, the same problem occurred. But the difficulty in getting an accurate number was not one of counting, but of the athlete's recovery. Usually, the athlete would have to slow down or stop to check the pulse, and this would cause the heart rate to diminish quickly, resulting in an inaccurate training heart rate.

There is another problem with manually taking your pulse. If you place your fingers on the carotid artery on the side of your neck, your pulse can easily be found. However, this area is also sensitive. Applying even moderate pressure here can significantly affect the heart rate, as well as blood flow to the brain and oxygen delivery. This is because the carotid area contains nerve endings which normally send messages to the brain indicating blood-pressure changes. Stimulating this area with pressure sends an improper message to the brain, which slows the heart, sometimes quite dramatically. Not only will this lower your heart rate significantly, it also can be dangerous. The oxygen debt created can cause fainting (or death in an extreme case).

The advent of heart monitors which sensed the heart rate directly from the chest wall was a great benefit. I was finally able to get accurate readings that matched ECG numbers without interrupting the athlete's workout.

Initially, athletes would use the monitor once per week, while running on the track or while riding a bike. They would come to my clinic where we would strap the monitor on and they would go out for a workout. At the same time, I would observe the athlete's gait (posture during the workout) and correlate the mechanical efficiency with the heart rate.

During these assessment sessions, I was able to give the athlete a better idea of how fast, or slow, he or she should be training. It soon became evident that the athletes needed more consistent training quality, rather than them relying on the feel of the workout on the day they used the heart monitor. Soon it became necessary for each athlete to have his or her own heart monitor and train with it every day. Some bought their own monitors and used them during each workout.

One of the most significant observations I made was that athletes who wore heart-rate monitors during each workout felt better, and improved in performance at a faster rate than others who trained without a monitor.

Up until this time, the training heart rate we chose was based on how the athlete looked during my assessments on the track or road. Previous to that I knew that the number I found to be ideal in my assessment was different than the standard formula traditionally promoted — the 220 formula.

Using this formula, the athlete determines the training heart rate by subtracting his or her age from 220 to get the maximum heart rate. In reality, most athletes who obtain their maximum heart rate by pushing themselves to exhaustion will find it is probably not 220 minus their age. About a third will find their maximum is above this heart rate, a third will be below and only a third may be close to 220 minus their age. This "maximum heart rate" is then multiplied by either a percentage of VO_2 max or a percentage of estimated maximum heart rate ranging from 65 to

85 percent. These two percentage levels are very different, and patients sometimes interchange them. In addition, the percentage most athletes choose is the higher option rather than a lower one, since most athletes feel the need to train with more intensity to obtain benefits

Since everyone is unique, the 220 formula made little sense to me, as it relies on an estimated maximum heart rate and training at a specified percentage of that number based on very subjective evidence. I have observed that this equation fits only about 35 percent of individuals. The variations may be due to age, resting heart rate, body weight, and other factors. Using chronological age may not be the best approach, as an athlete's physiological age should also be taken into consideration.

As the number of athletes I worked with increased, it was necessary to find another method of determining which heart rate was best for a given athlete. More clues would come from laboratory information.

The respiratory quotient (RQ) is the ratio of fat to sugar used for fuel during activity. By measuring RQ and correlating that with the heart rate, it became easier to obtain an ideal training heart rate for a given athlete.

These numbers were correlated with the ones determined from empirical data I made on the track or road, where the only assessment was the observation of gait. It was obvious to me that the most efficient mechanical movement of the athlete during an endurance workout correlated with a high percentage of fat-burning. (This is not to be construed as the highest percentage of fat-burning, which would be associated with the lowest levels of training.)

Training for endurance requires high amounts of fat-burning, with more of it needed for increased endurance. In time, other vital observations were made. The relationship between training at the prescribed heart rate and the ability to burn more fat at the same heart rate became apparent, as well as the relationship of these changes to a lowered RQ and an increased speed.

Even more important was the fact that by incorporating training at higher heart rates too often, the same progress did not follow. In other words, increased fat-burning would usually not occur. This combined well with the theory promoted by New Zealand coach Arthur Lydiard, who said endurance athletes needed to build an aerobic base to improve performance.

Still missing was the ability for anyone to determine maximum aerobic heart rate, as I now called it. Training at this heart rate would improve endurance and performance, while allowing the athlete to burn more fat as fuel and improve overall health. This meant a new formula had to be created, one which took into account as many factors as possible, including the individual athlete's uniqueness.

5

The 180 Formula

Traditionally, athletes have used the "talk test," or the 220 formula to determine their aerobic training levels. My 180 Formula replaces both.

You may be familiar with the talk test, which assumes you are exercising within your aerobic range if you can comfortably talk to your training partners during a workout. This test is not reliable, and often results in someone training in a mild anaerobic state for weeks or months before the person realizes it.

It's better to use a formula which is not only more sensible, but more scientific: the 180 Formula. This method considers physiological as well as chronological age. It is based on the theory that training allows aerobic progress while establishing or maintaining balance in all other systems of the body. As such, use of the formula not only is an effective training approach but also adds a therapeutic component to your program.

180 Formula

1. Subtract your age from 180 (180 – age).
2. Modify this number by selecting among the following categories the one that best matches your health and fitness profile:

   a. If you have or are recovering from a major illness (heart disease, any operation, any hospital stay, etc.) or are on any regular medication (discussed later), subtract an additional 10.

b. If you have been inconsistent with exercise, have been exercising with injury, have regressed in training or competition, get more than two colds or bouts of flu per year, or have allergies, or if you have not exercised before, subtract an additional 5.

c. If you have been exercising regularly (at least four times weekly) for up to two years without any of the problems just mentioned, keep the number (180 – age) the same.

d. If you are a competitive athlete who has been training for more than two years without any of the problems listed and have made progress in competition without injury, add 5.

For example, if you are 30 years old and fit into category b, you get the following:

$$180 - 30 = 150. \text{ Then } 150 - 5 = 145 \text{ bpm}$$

In this example, exercising at a heart rate of 145 beats per minute will be highly aerobic, allowing you to properly and maximally develop endurance. Above that, there's a rapid change to more anaerobic function, exemplified by a shift to burning more sugar and less fat for fuel.

Initially, training at this relatively low rate may be stressful for many athletes. "I just can't train that slowly!" is a common comment. But after a short time, you will feel better and your pace will quicken at that same heart rate. You will not be stuck training at that relatively slow pace for too long. Still, for many athletes it is difficult to change bad habits.

If it is difficult to decide which of two groups best fits you, choose the group or outcome that results in the lowest heart rate. In athletes who are taking medication that may affect the heart rate, those who wear a pacemaker, or those who have special circumstances not discussed here, further individualization with the help of a practitioner or specialist may be necessary.

The heart rate obtained with this formula is referred to as the maximum aerobic heart rate and is used for the MAF Test (discussed later) and for all aerobic training. This heart rate is usually lower, sometimes significantly lower, than when the traditional 220 formulas are used.

The 180 Formula may need to be further individualized for people over the age of 65. For these patients, up to 10 beats may have to be added, depending on individual levels of health and fitness. This does not mean just add 10, but an honest self assessment is important.

For athletes 16 years of age and under, the formula is not applicable; rather, a heart rate of 165 bpm may be best. A lower heart rate based on the individual's health and fitness may occasionally be appropriate.

Once a maximum aerobic heart rate is found, a range from that number to 10 beats below that number should be used. For example, if an athlete's maximum aerobic heart rate is determined to be 155, that person's aerobic training zone would be 145 to 155 bpm. For the MAF test, the maximum aerobic heart rate is usually applied.

Case History

Don was a good athlete who usually placed in the top of his age group. When he came to my clinic with chronic injuries, fatigue and recurrent colds, one of the first things we did was test him on the track with a heart monitor. At his maximum aerobic heart rate, Don was only able to run at an 8:40 pace — almost 2 minutes slower than his usual training pace! I recommended that Don train at this pace with a monitor for a three-month base period. But two weeks later he called me and said it was impossible to run that slow. I again explained the whole process and how he would get faster. A week later he faxed a letter saying he could not train by my recommendations. Several months later, Don came back to the clinic with more serious symptoms. Now he was ready to train aerobically. It took several more months for Don to increase his aerobic pace until finally he was running his "normal" 6:45 pace — but this time at a heart rate that was 25 beats slower.

Most heart-rate monitors can be set for different ranges, providing you with an audible indication if your heart rate goes over or under your preset levels. Set yours at the maximum aerobic rate you determined. If your max aerobic heart rate is 145, the monitor would be set for a maximum pulse of 145 on the high rate, and 135 for the low rate. This gives you a comfortable range for your workout.

A frequently asked question by multisport athletes is, should different heart rates be used for different endurance sports? The answer is no. The 180 Formula holds true for all aerobic training activities. At the same heart rate, different endurance sports require the same levels of metabolic activity. So whether you're swimming, biking or running, many physiologic parameters are the same.

However, other aspects are quite different when comparing swimming, for example, to running. One significant difference is perceived exertion, which is a subjective feeling the athlete has in relation to the workout. Another difference, a very objective one, is gravity stress. The difference in this stress between swimming and running is dramatic; there is very little gravity influence in the water, but that same force is maximally affecting the body during running. A great deal of energy may not have to go into countering gravity stress in the pool but just the opposite is true during a run.

As a result, the heart rate during swimming is usually lower compared to running at the same effort, since the stress level is diminished in the water. Another way of looking at this phenomenon is to compare perceived exertion at the same heart rate. Swimming at a heart rate of 145 feels more difficult compared to running at the same heart rate, which feels relatively easy. (This is true if you're equally trained in both disciplines.)

In relation to the stress of swimming and running, cycling falls between the two, along with cross-country skiing, skating and most other endurance activities. In these actions, there is some gravity stress along with mechanical stress.

Another factor that influences the heart rate is technique. For the beginning swimmer, the heart rate is usually much higher. As you become more proficient, the stress level lowers and the same intensity results in lower heart rates.

The benefits of training with a heart monitor are many, and only with time and experience will you come to truly appreciate them.

Another significant benefit of applying the 180 Formula to heart-rate training is the chemical response by the body to training at that relatively lower level of intensity.

Normally, the body produces chemicals called oxygen free radicals in response to many stresses, including certain types of training. While these chemicals can be helpful, too many contribute to degenerative problems such as inflammatory conditions, heart disease and cancer. In addition, increased free radicals speed the aging process.

High intensity anaerobic training produces large amounts of free radicals. This is the reason some professionals suggest limiting your training. But even moderate training intensities can produce free radicals. However, using the 180 Formula as your guide, free-radical production is minimized. Studies show that training at this efficient intensity is ideal when free-radical stress is a concern.

6

The MAF Test

One of the many benefits of the MAF Program is that you will generate more speed with the same effort. This is true not only of training speed but race pace as well. Another advantage of using a heart-rate monitor is the ability to objectively measure these improvements using the Maximum Aerobic Function Test, or MAF Test.

The MAF Test objectively measures the improvements you make in aerobic speed due to the progress made by the aerobic system during base-building. Without objective measurements, you run the risk of fooling yourself into thinking all is well with training.

The MAF Test can be performed with any endurance activity. Your goal is to measure how fast you can run, bike, swim, skate, etc. at your aerobic maximum heart rate. Or, how far you can go in a given time frame at the same heart rate.

During the MAF Test, use your maximum aerobic heart rate found by using the 180 Formula previously described. While working out at that heart rate, determine some parameter such as pace (minutes per mile), speed (miles per hour) or repetitions (i.e., laps in a pool) over time. The test can also be done on stationary equipment measuring watts.

If you want to test your maximum aerobic function during running, for example, perform the test on a track by running at your maximum aerobic heart rate. Running from three to five miles provides more information, although a one-mile test still has value. The test should always be done following a warm-up. The following is an actual MAF Test example performed by running on a track, calculating time in minutes per mile:

Mile 1	8:21
Mile 2	8:27
Mile 3	8:38
Mile 4	8:44
Mile 5	8:49

As indicated above, it is normal to obtain slightly slower times with each ensuing mile. The slower your first mile, the more the time will slow between the first and fifth mile. For example, if your first mile is 10:17 pace, your fifth mile may turn out to be 11:20. On the other hand, if your first mile is faster, the difference between miles one and five is less. For example, if your first mile is 5:50, your fifth mile may be 6:14.

During any one MAF Test, your times should always get slower; the first mile should always be the fastest, and the last the slowest. If that's not the case, it usually means your warm-up was inadequate. An example of this is if your first mile is 7:46 and your second is 7:39.

In addition, as the weeks pass, the MAF Test should show faster times compared to previous tests. For example, over several months, we can see the endurance progress in this actual case:

	April	May	June	July
Mile 1	8:21	8:11	7:57	7:44
Mile 2	8:27	8:18	8:05	7:52
Mile 3	8:38	8:26	8:10	7:59
Mile 4	8:44	8:33	8:17	8:09
Mile 5	8:49	8:39	8:24	8:15

However, this improvement is usually evident only during the aerobic base-building part of your training program. During periods of anaerobic training, including periods of competitions, improvement in time usually slows or stops. The reasons are discussed in a later chapter.

Performing the MAF Test on a bike is similar, except on your bike you have a couple of effective ways to record the test. The best and easiest method is to pick a flat bike course that takes about 30 to 45 minutes to complete. Following a warm-up, ride at your maximum aerobic heart rate, and record exactly how long it takes to ride the test course. As you progress, your times should get lower. Riding your course today, for example, may take 36 minutes and 50 seconds. In three weeks it may take you 35:30 and in another three weeks 34:15. After three months of base work, the same course may only take you 33 minutes flat.

Another option is to ride on a flat course and see how fast a pace you can maintain while holding your heart rate at your maximum aerobic level. This works best in a velodrome, or indoors on a trainer or rollers. As you progress, your speed should increase. If you start at 18 mph, for example, following a three-month period of building aerobic base, you could be riding 24 mph at the same heart rate.

Perform the MAF Test regularly, throughout the year, and chart your results. I recommend doing the test every three to four weeks. More often than that may result in mental stress; aerobic speed will usually not improve significantly within one week. Focusing on the test this often can foster an obsession much like that seen in athletes who are addicted to weighing themselves on the scale daily or even more often.

Performing the test irregularly or not often enough defeats one of its purposes — knowing when your training is going off course. If something interferes with your progress — training, diet, stress, etc. — you don't want to wait until you're feeling badly or racing poorly to find that out. Loss of health and fitness will be apparent from your MAF Test, and can be assessed this way sometimes long before you get symptoms.

One of the great benefits of the MAF Test is its ability to objectively inform you of an obstacle long before you feel it or see it as an injury or declining performance. As with any evaluation, an important element of the MAF Test is knowing what is normal and what is not. During endurance training, you could encounter three different phases: progression, plateau and regression.

As I have said repeatedly, if you successfully develop your aerobic system you will generate more aerobic speed. This is the progressive phase of the program, and it can and should continue for many years without regression. However, this period may have phases of normal plateaus. Initially, your progress will be measured by large improvements — less minutes per mile, more miles per hour or whatever parameters you choose to use. As time goes on and development continues, progress occurs at a slower rate. The following graph represents actual progress of an age-group cyclist over a four-year period. Notice the plateaus scattered throughout the period.

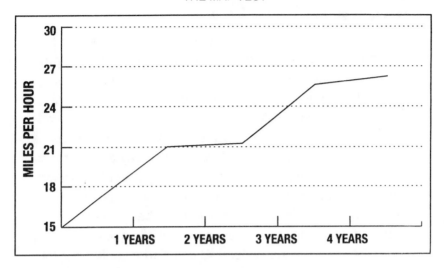

There are actually two different kinds of plateaus. One is normal and the other unhealthy.

With improvement, you will eventually arrive at a normal leveling off — almost as if your body needs a rest from the progress it is making. The reason for this is unclear, although it seems like the metabolic, neurological and muscular aspects of the body require a period of adjustment. It may also be related to the need for recovery, much like ascending a long hill. These normal plateaus should not last too long — a few weeks to a month or two at most. At the end of that time, progress should again resume as measured by the MAF Test. If you stay on a plateau for longer periods, it may be abnormal.

An abnormal plateau is due to some obstacle which prevents progress. The MAF Test is very useful to help diagnose an abnormal plateau. Once you find your times have stayed the same for too long, the next step is to find out why. Specifically, what is interfering with your progress. There could be many factors.

By far the most common reason for an abnormal plateau is stress. Recall that stress can be physical, chemical or mental. Typically, some lifestyle stress, often more than one, will cause your body to plateau. The weather may also be a stress which can halt endurance progression.

Case History

Karen's progress was rapid, almost from the moment she began the program. Her first mile MAF Test on the track went from 9:07 pace in September to 7:52 the following June. However, following that improvement, there was a long three-month plateau. Finally, progress was restored. The next year the same pattern was evident: Her great progress halted abruptly and was followed by three months of no improvements. At first I thought Karen's plateaus were normal. Eventually, I considered the possibility that perhaps her tolerance to the summer weather — hazy, hot and humid conditions — was too much of a stress, and this was the cause of the plateau. Since Karen could not go to the mountains for the summer to avoid the weather stress, we cut her training schedule down by about 30 percent. Using that strategy beginning in the late spring, Karen continued progressing through the next summer. She also felt better than normal, and continued racing better than the previous year.

If you think your plateau is abnormal, assess yourself carefully, or get help from a professional who understands the needs of endurance athletes. Find out what is blocking your natural progress. In addition to stress, other types of progress-halting stress include overtraining, dehydration, poor diet and nutritional problems.

Even worse than not making progress is regressing. Indeed, that is just what happens if your plateau is prolonged. An abnormal plateau resulting from some type of stress or factors mentioned above will eventually cause your MAF Test to get worse each time you check it. If this happens, your body is in a "red alert" and you should be very cautious. This is the time when you become most vulnerable to injury and ill health. In this case, one recommended strategy is to cut your training by 50 percent. This will ensure more rest and recovery. Another suggestion is to stop all anaerobic workouts, including racing. For some athletes, cutting both duration and intensity are worthy of serious consideration.

In addition, reassess your training, racing, life stresses, and so on. Find out why the natural progress which should be taking place has been thrown into reverse.

During the early stages of regression you may not necessarily feel bad or notice an injury. Those obvious signs and symptoms occur in the later stages of deteriorating endurance. There may not be any early symptoms. Even blood tests may appear normal. The only sign that something is wrong may come from your MAF Test.

If you do not respect the advice of your body, which during the MAF Test indicated you were regressing, you may ultimately be seeking first-aid advice from a professional. This could be due to exhaustion, injury, sickness or some other major breakdown, possibly including one on a mental level. Regressing endurance parallels poor health.

A decline in endurance is so common that many athletes and coaches think it's normal. Well, it's not. This common notion has given birth to the myth of "the peak." This belief asserts that you build up your ability, progress to a high level where race performance is at its highest, then you fall off. When you decline from this peak, you perform poorly.

Rather than the philosophy of a peak, I promote one of continued improvement throughout the race year, with each race better than the next. But can we really analyze endurance races that closely? I don't think so. Each competition has with it so many variables: weather, travel factors, different terrain and so on. So rather than focusing on analyzing something as subjective as the race, focus on getting as healthy and fit as you can, and use the MAF Test to objectively measure progress.

The MAF Test can be applied to any endurance activity. While it is not a classic double-blind scientific study, it still maintains the reproducibility important for objective, ongoing evaluations.

However, there are a number of factors which may affect your test results. When running, for example, the type of track surface may have a slight influence on your pace. The modern high-tech track surfaces result in the fastest pace, whereas the old cinder tracks will slow your pace at the same heart rate. Uneven tracks will give slower times compared to perfectly flat surfaces. The ideal situation is to have an indoor track. But beware, too short a track will generally cause a slightly slower pace due to the increased turning.

On your bike, a velodrome is ideal but not accessible for most athletes. The roughness or smoothness of the road surface, its varying grades, and traffic will all affect your test results. The net result of hills usually is a worsening of pace, unless there are significantly more downhills. A good option is to use a wind trainer or rollers.

Usually, these factors, and the others described below, can make a difference of five to eight seconds per mile on a track, or two to three miles per hour on your bike, possibly more. But to ensure the MAF Test is most accurate, be consistent: Use the same course or method each time you perform the test. In the event that you change your test course, be sure to note it in your diary or chart.

Other factors which may potentially interfere with your test include the weather, altitude, hydration and your equipment. Most of these factors can work against you by increasing your physical effort, which increases the heart rate. Since you are working at a specific heart rate, the result is a slower pace. Again, the minimal amount of influence should not pose a real problem. Rather, you should just be aware of these factors.

The weather influences your body, and therefore the MAF Test, in several ways:

- A headwind may physically counter your forward motion, raising your heart rate. A tailwind will have the opposite effect — you'll go faster at the same heart rate.

- Temperature may also be a factor during your test. Extremes of heat and cold will raise your heart rate, forcing you to slow down.

- High humidity can act much like a headwind. It is a physical barrier of water which you must work through. The increased effort raises your heart rate and results in a slower test.

- Rain and snow are similar to humidity and headwinds. Going through rain (and to a lesser extent snow) requires more effort. In addition, if the surface you are on is wet with water or, especially, covered with snow, additional physical effort is required.

- Barometric pressure can also have a slowing effect on your MAF Test. Low barometric pressure results in a slightly lower oxygen uptake. The result is less oxygen gets to your muscles and your body compensates by raising the heart rate.

Often, weather stress is not the result of a single factor. A combination of cold and wind, for example, can elevate the heart rate significantly. Summer heat, humidity and low pressure, sometimes referred to as the "dog days of August," can also stress your body and raise the heart rate. For these reasons, if you arrive at your MAF Test day and the weather is extreme, wait a day or more until the weather stress has lessened.

Altitude can have a significant effect on the body and MAF Test, especially if you have not had a chance to adapt to a new altitude. If you're headed for the mountains to train for a period of time, wait at least a week or more until you adjust to the altitude before performing your MAF Test. Even then, your times generally slow when you ascend to higher altitudes. When descending to lower altitudes, your MAF Test improves.

Hydration also affects your aerobic pace. Even slight dehydration can slow you down. Once you dehydrate, it may take 24 hours or longer to rehydrate, no matter how much water you consume. It's important to drink smaller amounts of water all day rather than large amounts a couple of times a day.

Your equipment can also affect the outcome of your MAF Test. The two most significant items are your bike and running shoes.

Your bike set-up and positioning, the pressure and wear on your tires, and any other factors that change drag, such as clothing, can slow your MAF Test results. Make a note in your diary if your test is done with a different bike set-up, more clothing or other factors that may change the test.

Running shoes will also affect the results of your MAF Test. In general, shoes with more cushioning and more support, and heavier shoes all slow you down. Lighter shoes, including racing styles, generally allow you to run faster at the same heart rate.

While most of the above factors will raise your heart rate and slow your pace or speed, performing the MAF Test for longer rather than shorter times will help compensate for these natural variables. For running, this means 5 miles, for a bike test, a total of about 30 to 45 minutes or more.

One other factor that will affect your MAF Test is worth mentioning here: ill health. When you are sick, your body's immune system is working very hard to recover, and it needs all the energy it can get. The last thing your body wants to do is work out, especially when you have an elevated temperature. In this situation, don't train or race. If you've ever attempted this, and worn a heart monitor, you know what happens; your heart rate elevates, sometimes drastically. The same effect is observed if you are anemic; less oxygen can be delivered to the muscles, with the resulting MAF Test results being slower.

Some Factors which Affect the MAF Test

Factor	Effect
Running Surfaces	
All-weather	improves
Dirt, grass, cinder	worsens
Indoor	improves
400-meter	improves
200-meter	worsens
Bike or Skate	
Velodrome	improves
Smooth road	improves
Rough road	worsens
Hills	worsens
Weather	
Wind	worsens
Rain/snow	worsens
Humidity	worsens
Low barometric pressure	worsens
Very high/low temperature	worsens
Altitude	
Higher	worsens
Lower	improves

Another important aspect of the MAF Test is that it is indicative of performance. A direct relationship exists between your aerobic pace and race effort. In other words, as your MAF Test improves, so will your racing ability.

In the early 1980s, I collected a lot of MAF data on runners. Back then, I called it maximum aerobic pace (MAP), but as all other types of athletes began to use the test, "pace" was changed to "function." However, the data runners provided was more objective because we could control more variables.

After hundreds of tests and several racing seasons, it was evident that the pace a runner could perform at his or her aerobic maximum pace was positively correlated with race pace. The race distances varied, but more data was gathered for 5K and 10K distances. The chart below, based on actual data, is an example of the relationship between MAF and 5K race performance.

Through the years it also became obvious that performance in all endurance events — triathlons, marathons, cycling events, swimming — could be improved by developing a faster aerobic pace. Even athletes involved in basketball, soccer, tennis and other events that required significant amounts of aerobic efforts could improve.

MAF and Performance (Minutes per Mile)

MAF Pace	5K Race Pace	5K Time
10:00	7:30	23:18
9:00	7:00	21:45
8:30	6:45	20:58
8:00	6:30	20:12
7:30	6:00	18:38
7:00	5:30	17:05
6:30	5:15	16:19
6:00	5:00	15:32
5:45	4:45	14:45
5:30	4:30	13:59
5:15	4:20	13:28
5:00	4:15	13:12

A note for multisport athletes: If you are training for more than one or two events, you may frequently be at a plateau for one event. For example, if you are measuring progress in swimming, biking and running, you may see your swim and run times improving while your bike improvement has reached a plateau. After a couple of months, this may change with swimming and cycling showing progress while your running maintains an even level. The reason for this is unclear, but I feel it is a normal part of progression.

The Big Picture

Are you confused with all the terminology? Don't worry, just follow the basic rules and your training will progress. Don't get caught up in the definitions; they don't all fit neatly together. That's not only true with my program, but also within the field of exercise physiology in general.

Two definitions which should be differentiated are maximum aerobic function and anaerobic threshold. They are obviously different states.

The maximum aerobic function is an endurance state where fat-burning is a significant part of the energy requirement. Often, in a properly trained athlete, fat is a significant fuel during MAF levels, sometimes accounting for up to 75 percent of the energy needs. As a result, there is less dependency on glucose for energy needs, and minimal lactic acid is produced. Generally, the percentage of maximum heart rate, which corresponds with the maximum aerobic level, is relatively low, usually about 70 percent, although this often varies with each athlete.

The definition of anaerobic threshold is the point at which the body's metabolism can no longer meet its energy demand predominantly by aerobic function. As a result, anaerobic metabolism increases significantly, along with lactic-acid production. Glucose becomes the primary fuel and fat-burning is greatly diminished. The percentage of maximum heart rate that corresponds to anaerobic threshold varies greatly, depending on training. It can be as high as 80 percent but can also be below 70 percent. The chart below incorporates these concepts, along with some others, including respiratory quotient.

TRAINING LEVELS	% MAX HR	SUBSTRATE UTILIZATION (% Carbo and Fat)		
Max HR	100	Max	Min	Higher
Max Anaerobic Training	90	↑	↑	↑
Anaerobic Threshold (Lactate Threshold)	Varies	GLUCOSE	FAT	RQ
Aerobic Maximum	Varies			
Warm Up/Cool Down	Varies	↓	↓	↓
Recovery	Varies	Min	Max	Lower

7

Stress and the Athlete

E xcess stress is not only the most common problem I see in athletes, it's also the problem most neglected and underestimated by them. Stress is such an important aspect of, and influence on, training and competition that I include it early in this book. Understanding what stress is will help you more effectively manage and avoid it. And that will greatly help your effort to get healthy (function optimally without injury) and fit (perform better).

Stress can be defined as any factor that affects the body (or mind) which causes the body to react and adapt. This reaction and adaptation is managed to a large extent by the adrenal glands, located on top of each kidney. These glands are also responsible for recovery from the stress of training and competition. The response to stress takes time and energy, with more stress requiring more time and energy to properly adapt.

Stress can come from anywhere — your job, family, other people. It comes in the form of emotions, infections, allergic reactions, physical trauma and exertion, and the weather. But not all stress is negative. Since stress is a factor that evokes a reaction in the body, the outcome may also be positive. Your workout is an example. By stressing your muscles and metabolism, the end result over time is that your body performs better. But that same stressor — your workout — can turn to a negative if you go too far beyond the body's ability to recover.

We can categorize stress on three levels: physical, chemical and mental. Physical stress includes your workout, bodily strain at your job site, such as sitting at a desk all day, prolonged driving in a car or truck, or heavy lifting. Wearing improper training shoes or riding a bike not set up correctly for your body are also common physical stresses.

Chemical stress can adversely affect the body as well. Improper nutrition, dehydration, and too much caffeine are typical examples. Body chemistry controls most bodily functions, including the nervous system and brain, muscles and the intestines. So these areas are especially sensitive to chemical stress.

Most people think of stress in its mental form. Tension, anxiety and depression are common examples. But unrealistic athletic goals, not understanding or having knowledge about even simple things like your bike set up, or tension over airline travel are also familiar stresses.

More often people have stress from more than one category, and frequently from a combination of all three types. And, stress is cumulative. The response to a physical stress from a Sunday race may be amplified by a chemical stress on Monday and further compounded with a mental stress on Tuesday. All of which will affect your training on Wednesday through Friday, and finally your Saturday race.

The weather is also a potential stressor, with certain people more vulnerable. Weather stress may affect us physically, chemically or mentally. Extremes in temperatures or humidity, very low barometric pressure, and the sun are illustrations. Because of weather stress, training or racing in these environments usually has adverse effects on your body and performance.

One distinguishing feature of many top athletes is their ability to tolerate stress. A small part of this coping mechanism of the adrenal glands may be genetic. But those without strong adrenals still have an option: stress control.

The key to controlling stress is to first carefully assess it, with the goal of diminishing or eliminating some of your stress. This includes strategies such as making a list of all your stress, to testing your adrenal hormones.

The first step is to make a list of all your stress, taking several days to complete it (you won't think of all your different stresses right away). Then separate that list into two parts. Make the "A" list from stresses you can eliminate or control. This may include unhealthy eating habits like rushing your meals, to trying to get a few more miles out of your already worn-out shoes. The "B" list is composed of stresses you can't control very well. This may include job stress or the weather. In reality, almost any stress can be modified or eliminated. It's a question of how far you want to go to eliminate stress.

Once you can "see" your stress on paper, it will be easier to manage. Start with your "A" list stresses first because you have control over them — not that it's always easy. You may be able to improve on some and totally eliminate others. Some will require habit changes. In all, it's a big task, but one that will return great benefits.

Then there's the "B" list of stress; if there's nothing you can do about them anyway, don't worry about them. By regulating the stress on your "A" list, your adrenal glands will have a much easier time managing the ones on your "B" list.

In addition to making your stress lists, you're probably familiar with other strategies for dealing with stress. But for many of you, most of the time you don't use them. Here's a reminder of some of them:

- Just say "no" when asked to do something you really don't want to do.

- Decide not to waste your present time over the past, or worry about the future. (That's not to say you should ignore the past or not plan for the future.)

- Learn some relaxation techniques, and perform them regularly.

- When you're concerned about something, or when a problem comes up, talk it over with someone you trust.

- Simplify your life. Start by eliminating trivia.

- Prioritize your busy schedule; do the most important things first.

What's most important to understand about stress is that too much of it interferes with rest. Or more accurately, excess stress requires more rest. And if you don't have enough rest, your training is adversely affected. In many ways, stress is also like work. Here again, too much stress, like work, interferes with training.

Case History

Janet owned a business, had a family and was a triathlete. Fitting training for all three activities into her schedule was always more of a challenge than racing. She complained that stress was her main problem but brushed it aside saying it was part of life. For Janet, listing all her stress on paper was a frightening experience, but a revelation. Janet was able to eliminate and modify many little problems from her day. Over the next few months, she got her kids to do more of the work at home, hired a new office manager, and did many workouts around her schedule instead of everyone else's. Eventually, Janet not only felt better, but her performances also improved.

A common stress, a mental one, is obsession. I'm not talking about compulsive disorders or other more obvious and extreme problems, but the common obsessions many of us harbor. Too often, these "mental fixations" overrun the rational mind when it comes to training. A frequent example may be your Sunday workout with a group of athletes. You go out the door for an easy workout but without a real training plan, and follow the group. But it usually turns out to be an obsessive race rather than the intended easy workout. Or, you complete a long hard race and a few days later you're asked to go for a long run with the group. You feel good and are almost obligated to go — and train too hard.

Another trademark of obsession is the fear that taking a day off will ruin all your training. Or somehow, you will lose benefits previously gained. This is often the case during a taper before a long race, and the days and weeks following a long hard effort.

Counting miles is another common obsession. At the end of your training week you tally up 38 miles; so, despite feeling tired, you run two extra miles just to get to 40. Or you jog the 80 meters from your car to the office twice daily and include that in your weekly mileage.

All these obsessions are significant stresses and can adversely affect your training, racing and health.

Since stress is regulated by the adrenals, high levels of stress keep these glands quite busy. This is a very significant aspect of training when you consider the other work your adrenal glands have to do.

The adrenal glands not only regulate stress and improve endurance and racing, but they are essential for life. These benefits are obtained through the action of hormones produced by the adrenals.

The glucocorticoids, which include cortisol, are an important group of adrenal hormones with several actions. They have anti-inflammatory actions, which you need on a daily basis if you train. Even an easy workout can produce some inflammation from wear and tear. Without the adrenals' control over this process, the inflammation would persist, ultimately preventing you from training. Cortisol also helps make fat more available for energy, sparing glucose in the process, and it stimulates protein utilization necessary for repair and recovery.

The mineralocorticoids help regulate your electrolytes, especially sodium and potassium. Aldosterone, the main mineralocorticoid, keeps sodium in the body. In this process, water levels are more easily maintained, and this counters the potential for dehydration.

Epinephrine and norepinephrine are two other important adrenal hormones. They increase the rate and power of the heartbeat, increase metabolism, and help release sugar and fat for energy use. These hormones also improve circulation in the working muscles, partly by increasing blood pressure and increasing respiration.

Many of the adrenal hormones increase with training intensity. But too much adrenal activity can pose a problem. For example, too much cortisol suppresses the immune system. One symptom of overtraining is a lowered body-defense mechanism.

Adrenal activity functions like clockwork, and is referred to as your circadian rhythm. A change in time zones, which may take place when you fly east or west, produces stress, with more produced with larger

Some Important Adrenal Hormones and their Actions

Hormone	Action
Glucocorticoids	Anti-inflammatory, increases fat-burning, spares glucose, promotes protein use
Mineralocorticoids	Regulates electrolytes and water
Epinephrine and Norepinephrine	Improves blood flow to muscles, promotes fat and glucose use

changes in time. The common symptom of "jet lag" results. You stay on your previous time schedule until the adrenal glands adapt to the stress, which may take several days depending on how far off your regular schedule you are. If you've ever competed several time zones away without first adapting, you probably understand this example of how stress works.

In the early part of this century, a young medical student named Hans Selye began to piece together the common triad of signs resulting from excess adrenal stress. They include adrenal-gland enlargement, depressed immunity and intestinal dysfunction. Selye eventually showed how the adrenals react to stress when confronted with an excess of it. This General Adaptation Syndrome has three distinct stages.

The three stages of adrenal reaction to stress begin with the alarm reaction, in which there is an increase in adrenal hormone production. This is an attempt by the adrenals to battle the increased stress. If it is successful, adrenal function returns to normal. But if over time the adrenals fail to meet the needs of the body to combat the stress, the adrenals enter the second phase called the resistance stage.

During this period, the adrenal glands themselves get larger, a process called hypertrophy. Since the increased hormone production could not counter the stress, the body decides to enlarge the whole gland as an attempt to do the same. If the stress is still not controlled, the adrenals enter the third stage, simply called exhaustion.

The exhaustion stage is just that: exhaustion. The adrenal glands are unable to adapt to stress. They have lost the war. As an endurance athlete, if you are in the exhaustion stage you may be considering retirement from racing and maybe even from training. At best you may be feeling quite badly and are struggling to figure out what's wrong. Maybe some well-meaning professional has provided a fancy name of a symptom, the end result of adrenal exhaustion, and this somehow makes you feel a bit at ease, having a name for what you feel.

In this exhaustion stage, the adrenals are unable to effectively counter the stress placed upon your body. At this point, the person usually becomes symptomatic — anything from physical and mental exhaustion to chronic injuries, from immune-system dysfunction and ulcers to other more serious health problems.

The General Adaptation Syndrome may take weeks, months or even years to build. As stated earlier, stress is cumulative. So unless the body can adapt well, adrenal stress can worsen over the years. Early symptoms commonly include fatigue and recurrent injuries, especially knee, low-back and foot problems. Also, dizziness upon standing, low blood pressure and allergies are typical.

The General Adaptation Syndrome	
1. alarm reaction	increased adrenal-hormone production
2. resistance stage	enlargement of the adrenal glands
3. exhaustion stage	adrenal glands unable to adapt to stress

In my practice, excess adrenal stress — or a lack of the adrenals to adapt to stress — was one of the most common problems found in endurance athletes. It may be due to overtraining, poor diet, work or family stress, or, as is most often the case, a culmination of all these stresses combined.

Whatever the problem, the cause of the excess adrenal stress, or why the glands could not counter existing stress, must be found and corrected. If you are successful, the body's natural endurance ability will be released and often progresses dramatically

Case History

Michael loved to run, but had chronic knee and low-back pain, allergies and intestinal problems which always interfered with his racing plans. He also had insomnia and could not get the rest he needed. He was a textbook case of a stressed athlete with matching symptoms. His diet revealed a large amount of sugar consumption, about 9 cups of coffee a day and no breakfast. And, he worked about 60 hours a week in a very physical job. Michael wanted to qualify for the Boston Marathon. But my concern was for his overall health. His blood pressure and cholesterol were too high, and his weight and body fat were increasing each year. In the next 12 months, Michael successfully improved his health by eliminating coffee and sugar, eating a healthy diet and restricting his training. A year later he qualified for the Boston Marathon and ran a time of 2:54.

Stress Testing

Traditionally, stress testing is a screening procedure used to evaluate the heart under the tension of exercise. Most tests are done on treadmills, with bicycle ergometers and step tests used about 30 percent of the time.

Stress tests, when indicated, are done following a general evaluation that includes blood tests and an electrocardiogram (ECG). However, about 30 percent of those with normal ECGs have heart disease. Of these, only 80 percent can be diagnosed from a stress test.

One benefit of a stress test is that it may uncover a hidden hypertension in someone who has normal blood pressure at rest.

The American College of Sports Medicine's standard for those individuals who should undergo stress testing includes a person under the age of 35 with evidence of heart disease or a significant combination of risk factors. Primary risk factors include hypertension, hyperlipidemia and cigarette smoking. Secondary risk factors include family history, obesity and diabetes mellitus. It is generally not recommended that those under the age of 35 with no history or significant risk factors have a stress test.

Unfortunately, for most individuals with heart disease the most common first sign is death. And no one is immune, even athletes. But most risk factors are controllable, or at least easy to evaluate. Most athletes don't smoke, are active, and are not obese. These are three significant risk factors. Simple blood tests for total cholesterol (with HDL and LDL) and triglycerides can rule out hyperlipidemia, and blood glucose can rule out diabetes mellitus. Having a professional check your blood pressure occasionally can also help rule out hypertension.

Even endurance athletes who train regularly should pay attention to any signs or symptoms of possible heart disease. Thirty percent of the initial manifestation of heart disease is accompanied by angina pectoris. This pain is usually in the upper chest but often is displayed in the left shoulder or arm, neck and jaw. The cause is due to a low level of blood and oxygen through the coronary artery, the main blood vessel of the heart. The symptom usually begins during activity and subsides with rest.

Stress tests are also not highly accurate. About 25 percent of tests yield false-negative results, meaning the test results have not uncovered an existing problem. In 15 percent of tests, there is a false-positive result, meaning it indicated a problem which does not exist; this leaves 60 percent of the tests accurate.

8

The Overtraining Syndrome

O vertraining has been traditionally described as diminished performance that results from an increase in training volume and/or intensity. I previously discussed overtraining as an imbalance in our simple equation Training = Workout + Recovery. This may result from excess number and/or intensity of workouts, lack of recovery, or both. This multifactorial problem is referred to as the overtraining syndrome and is associated with neurological (i.e., sympathetic and parasympathetic imbalance), metabolic (i.e., adrenal, nutritional and dietary problems), and muscular signs and symptoms.

Prevention and correction of the overtraining syndrome begins with assessment. Observing the subtle symptoms in their earliest stages are crucial to the prevention of further regression. The MAF Test is a powerful tool for assessing overtraining as it begins to develop, and may provide the first objective sign. In order for this assessment to be effective, you must conduct the MAF Test every three to four weeks.

I would like to discuss the full spectrum of overtraining, not just the more obvious late-stage conditions. The overtraining syndrome can be described as three stages:

- **Functional Overtraining.** The onset and earliest stage where very subtle indicators can clue you in that you're heading for more serious problems.

- **Sympathetic Overtraining.** Where an overactivity of certain nervous and hormonal factors cause a variety of signs and symptoms.

- **Parasympathetic overtraining.** A stage resulting from the exhaustion of nervous and hormonal factors which also drag down muscle function.

The overtraining syndrome typically results in poor performance and structural injury. In addition, secondary chemical injuries such as fatigue and infection, as well as altered mood states and reproductive function, are evident. Note that the diminished performance associated with overtraining does not occur only in competitive athletes; it is also seen in people performing everyday chores.

An athlete's lifestyle may also contribute to overtraining; this aspect of overtraining was recognized as early as 1923. To date, however, mainstream medicine has not produced a standard assessment or treatment process for the full spectrum of overtraining, perhaps because research on overtraining has yielded variable results, making the syndrome difficult to understand using that approach. For example, some studies demonstrate that performance reduction is associated with high cortisol levels from the adrenal glands, whereas others do not show this relationship. It is evident that overtraining is a highly individual problem, the onset of which is subtle (functional) and often ignored or not recognized. It produces not just physical signs and symptoms, but various complaints that are without organic disease.

Functional Overtraining

A MAF Test that demonstrates an abnormal plateau or regression, as compared to the normal plateau and progress, may be the first sign of overtraining. This first stage is referred to as functional overtraining because it is not accompanied by classical problems but by very subtle, or subclinical ones. Interestingly, it is sometimes accompanied by a sudden and dramatic improvement in competitive performance that may convince you that training is progressing well. This temporary improvement may be due to an abnormally increased sympathetic function.

Another problem associated with functional overtraining is an imbalance between aerobic and anaerobic function. While this may be determined by a professional through a proper history, exam or other tests, anyone can compare his or her maximum aerobic function and maximum anaerobic function. Recall that aerobic function can be measured with the MAF Test and anaerobic function by competitive performance or time trial. An imbalance is evident, for example, if you can perform the MAF Test at 7 minutes/mile but run a 5 or 10K race under 5 minutes/mile. It is not uncommon for talented athletes to compete at high levels but achieve proportionately slow scores on their MAF Test. Other athletes, such as cyclists may find the traditional time trial useful in this situation.

Functional overtraining probably is synonymous with overreaching, which has been shown in studies to boost performance but often turns into overtraining. Decreased performance levels are not evident until middle and later stages of overtraining, for example, during more obvious imbalance.

Functional overtraining may also be associated with adrenal gland dysfunction in its earliest stage as discussed in Chapter 7. In addition, it typically parallels aerobic deficiency. An understanding of adrenal dysfunction and aerobic deficiency, and the recognition of their functional symptoms, can be a significant deterrent against overtraining.

In addition to the above symptoms of overtraining, other problems begin in the functional overtraining period and continue through the second and third stage of overtraining. The may include fatigue, sleeping irregularities and hunger. It may also include the inability to lose that extra body fat, and occasionally an increase in body fat. Athletes may have difficulty getting out of bed, get sleepy after meals, and have an uncanny craving for sweets or caffeine. There are recurrent nutritional problems that often are due to a secondary malabsorption of nutrients, and excess consumption of carbohydrates is coupled with low fat and protein intakes.

Other complains common in those who are in the first stage of overtraining include:

- Increasing vulnerability to back, knee, ankle, and foot injuries.

- Adrenal gland dysfunction — typically a higher than normal cortisol, and lower testosterone and DHEA levels.

- Premenstrual syndrome and menopausal symptoms may be secondary complaints for women, but amenorrhea is the most common hormonal problem in overtrained women.

- Sexual dysfunction may be a problem for both sexes, typically producing reduced sexual desire and sometimes infertility.

- Mental and emotional stress, including mild or clinical depression and anxiety is not uncommon.

Sympathetic Overtraining

As overtraining progresses, the neurological imbalance worsens. Specifically, the sympathetic part of the nervous system becomes overactive. This results in the classic sign of an increased resting heart rate. Many athletes become aware of this if they regularly measure their morning heart rates. This is often associated with restlessness, and overexcitability. An increased training heart rate also emerges, producing a regression of MAF Test results — i.e., training at the same pace results in a higher heart rate, and if you're training at a given heart rate you have to slow down.

Sympathetic overtraining is more common in athletes who train with speed and power excess, those who train too often, those with contributing lifestyle stress, and most often those athletes who have a combination of these factors.

Dysfunction of the adrenal glands also progresses with sympathetic overtraining. This is why early detection and treatment of adrenal dysfunction is vital to the prevention of overtraining. Specific adrenal problems include various hormonal imbalances: cortisol output may rise to abnormal levels, further amplifying the normal elevation in cortisol that occurs prior to competition. The keen awareness and fine hand-to-eye coordination required in some sports are adversely affected by these hormone problems.

Generally, high cortisol levels have a catabolic effect on the system — this is comparable to that produced by exhaustive, prolonged training.

Measuring your cortisol levels may be one of the best tools to evaluate early overtraining.

High cortisol may also be associated with high insulin, and may be another sign of overtraining in some individuals. Moderate-intensity training usually suppresses insulin production during exercise, whereas studies show that maximal training intensities may increase the insulin response. This further increases the sympathetic nervous system activity and adds to the overtraining condition.

A good indicator of the anabolic/catabolic balance is the testosterone/cortisol ratio, with a reduction of 30 percent or more indicative of overtraining. Low testosterone levels, secondary to reduced DHEA, create significant problems for athletes because this hormone is important for muscle recovery and may help replace glycogen stores. The high cortisol associated with this stage of overtraining is also a significant problem. Fortunately, this hormone imbalance is relatively easily remedied (see *The ABCs of Hormonal Stress*).

Parasympathetic Overtraining

If the overtraining syndrome is allowed to progress, further hormonal and neurological imbalances occur. This continues to parallel adrenal dysfunction and aerobic deficiency. Eventually, the sympathetic nervous system becomes exhausted, and most if not all hormone levels are reduced. This is the third stage of overtraining, sometimes referred to as parasympathetic overtraining.

This stage is typically accompanied by decreased resting heart rates, lowered cortisol and other hormones, lack of desire to compete (and sometimes train), depression, and most notably exhaustion. Physical injuries are very common, and performance may diminish considerably. It also is associated with reduced lactate response, making lactate assessment inaccurate. The MAF Test has usually significantly regressed and plateaued at a poor level. This condition is associated with low resting heart rates and low heart-rate recovery from interval training or competition; some athletes misinterpret the low heart-rate recovery and think that they are improving.

The hormonal and neurological problems may result in increased sodium and chloride loss due to reduced aldosterone and may increase the athlete's vulnerability to hyponatremia — a condition of low sodium.

Overtraining and Amenorrhea

Menstrual dysfunction is frequently associated with overtraining, showing a positive correlation to high-intensity training. Overtrained female athletes often develop menstrual abnormalities including amenorrhea (the absence of menstrual bleeding), oligomenorrhea (a menstrual cycle between 35 and 90 days), and delayed menarche. This problem is individual and multifactorial; no clear single cause-and-effect pattern has been found between amenorrhea and training, diet, nutrition, psychiatric factors, or other factors not reviewed here.

The problems in many amenorrheic athletes may be considered a syndrome, comprising overtraining and disordered eating (especially reduced calorie intake and excessively low fat intake), excessively low body weight and body fat (especially femoral fat stores: fat around the hips, buttocks, and thighs), and vegetarianism.

One of the most significant structural problems associated with amenorrhea is bone loss. Overtraining results in low estrogen and progesterone levels, and this prolonged hormonal problem can decrease bone density and increase the risk of stress fractures, muscle soreness and physical fatigue. Demineralization of bone is most common in the spine, wrist and metatarsals, and scoliosis is also common. These imbalances can lead to structural problems in the skeleton later in life due to osteoporosis.

It should be noted that men may also have reduced hormones, specifically testosterone, which adversely affects bone density, also causing bone loss with many associated problems, including fractures.

Two significant chemical factors are associated with amenorrheic athletes: hormonal imbalance and nutritional deficiency. High cortisol and low DHEA, estrogen and progesterone levels are common in amenorrheic athletes. The reduced estrogen and progesterone profiles typical in amenorrheic athletes are actually very similar to those of post-menopausal women.

In many cases, amenorrheic athletes consume an energy-deficient diet. Laughlin and Yen (1996) state, "Growing evidence suggests that menstrual disturbances in female athletes are related to the metabolic cost of high levels of energy expenditure without compensatory increases in dietary intake." In some cases, however, amenorrheic athletes consume the same total kilocalories as those with normal menstrual cycles, but much less fat (up to 50 percent less) and protein, with higher carbohydrate intakes. Reduced fatty acid intakes can result in lower calcium absorption and lower bone calcium. This is typically aggravated by low dietary calcium intake but may be associated with normal blood levels of calcium.

Disordered eating itself is a complex mental/emotional issue, involving a full spectrum of problems from functional to pathological, and from poor eating, dieting, and preoccupation with low fat consumption to clinically diagnosed anorexia nervosa and bulimia. The endocrine equilibrium that regulates reproductive function can also be affected by other psychological factors; the stress associated with competition may be a significant variable as well.

In athletes without defined amenorrhea, other menstrual distress (so-called premenstrual syndrome) is nevertheless common and is also associated with increased consumption of carbohydrates (Johnson et al., 1995) and depression (O'Connor et al., 1989).

According to Dueck et al. (1996), non-pharmacological treatment can successfully re-establish normal hormonal profiles and menstrual activity in amenorrheic athletes.

Assessment and Treatment of Overtraining

When properly performed, the MAF Test is the most important evaluation an athlete can make to assess overtraining in its earliest stage. Also effective are hormone tests, such as the simple and accurate salivary cortisol, DHEA, and sometimes others as needed, such as testosterone, estrogen and progesterone.

An important tool for assessment of the functional overtraining and overtraining conditions that cannot be overemphasized is a good history — by yourself, a family member, or most accurately by a professional. The important questions that pertain to mood, energy levels, performance, and infections are important to answer honestly. These answers, combined with recent MAF test results, are crucial to discovering overtraining in its earliest stages.

Therapy for overtraining includes restructuring your training schedule, modifying lifestyle factors including diet and nutrition, and addressing stress. Finding a professional who can help is also a valuable adjunct. Although therapy should always be based on the assessment process, some specific avenues must be considered in athletes who are over-trained:

- The athlete should decrease training time by 50 to 70 percent, or more if necessary.

- The athlete should immediately cease all anaerobic training, including competition.

- A helpful remedy for an overtrained athlete is walking. Walking gently stimulates circulation and aerobic muscle fiber activity, and offers mental benefits much like those of meditation. It can also help redevelop the aerobic system — the first phase of retraining.

- Retraining, that is, building the aerobic base, should last three to six months and does not include any anaerobic training or competition.

Dietary and Nutritional Factors

Individual dietary and nutritional factors are important considerations in overtrained athletes, but because each athlete is unique, no overtraining protocol exists. However, some important issues should be considered.

Malabsorption is common in overtrained athletes, due to the high stress levels. Products such as betaine hydrochloride may improve digestion, and L-glutamine can improve nutrient absorption.

Overtrained athletes often experience a decreased plasma glutamine concentration, especially after long training sessions or competition. This can adversely affect immunity. Glutamine supplementation may improve both immune-system and small-intestine function.

Lifestyle stress, as discussed earlier, is important to consider as this stress may be as significant, or sometimes more significant, than training stress in overtrained athletes.

Caffeine consumption may be contraindicated for athletes who are overtrained. Reduction in or avoidance of stimulants such as coffee, tea, soda, and chocolate, as well as caffeine-containing, over-the-counter and prescription drugs, may be necessary.

Overtraining may disrupt the normal balance of eicosanoids, through which the inflammatory/anti-inflammatory state is balanced. This is one reason why overtrained athletes tend to have inflammatory-related injuries. Carefully evaluate the dietary fat ratios and consider the potential need for omega-3 supplementation.

Zinc may help reduce the abnormally high levels of cortisol common to overtrained athletes; however, timing is an important factor when one is supplementing with zinc. Cortisol should be measured throughout the day to determine abnormal peak levels; then the zinc supplements should be taken two to three hours prior to cortisol peaks.

Reduction of high-glycemic foods and consumption of smaller, more frequent meals may help those with abnormally high cortisol, especially those who have symptoms of depression. Moderating carbohydrate intake may also be helpful, as higher-carbohydrate diets may further elevate cortisol levels. Inadequate caloric intake and eating disorders may also adversely affect hormone balance.

Recurrent asthma symptoms (so-called exercise-induced asthma) may be an early indication of overtraining and usually respond well to choline supplementation and balanced training.

Recovery from Overtraining

Properly treated, athletes can often recover rapidly from overtraining imbalances. This is especially true in the functional overtraining stage. In this stage, modifying the training schedule, and making appropriate nutritional and dietary adjustments may do the trick. This rapid progress will be demonstrated in the MAF Test or other evaluations, including reductions in injuries and mental states. Usually, these athletes either will not need to modify their competitive schedules or will need to make only minor adjustments in near-term competitions.

Athletes in the second, sympathetic stage of overtraining can also respond quickly to proper recovery. However, those who have upcoming competitions may be required to modify or cancel those early events to allow for a more complete recovery from overtraining. However, building an acceptable aerobic base will take at least two and sometimes up to six months.

Those who are chronically overtrained and in the third parasympathetic stage respond much slower, even when the best care is available.

They may need to cancel their next competitive season (as if they had a physical injury that prevented competing) and spend time building their aerobic system, reducing stress, improving body chemistry through proper diet and nutrition, and learning about the body and its limits. These athletes will require six months or more, and sometimes a year or two, before resuming effective competition.

Because of the complex nature of an overtraining syndrome, it is not possible to formulate a specific approach to its remedy. Remember that a longer plateau in your MAF Tests may be the first sign of overtraining.

9

Hormones and Performance

Many common signs and symptoms — including named conditions — are typically associated with hormonal imbalance. In other words, when your hormones are not balanced, you get certain symptoms. And certain symptoms, or groups of symptoms called syndromes, have certain names. Premenstrual syndrome (PMS) is one common example.

Hormone imbalance results in a variety of problems. Ten common problems associated with hormonal imbalance are listed below. How many of the following problems do you have?

- **Overtraining.** A hormone profile can indicate, or even predict, an overtraining condition. For optimal athletic performance and prevention of the many problems associated with overtraining, use a salivary hormone test at least twice a year (beginning and mid-season) and make appropriate training adjustments. Cortisol, DHEA and testosterone are the best indicators of training efficiency for athletes.

- **Poor recovery.** The lack of recovery is often due to hormone imbalance — this may be associated not only with training and competition, but any physical work (such as yard or housework), or a stressful day at the office. Low testosterone often accompanies this problem, but it's often preceded by high cortisol and low DHEA.

- **Reduced fat-burning and poor weight regulation.** These are associated with specific hormone imbalance, especially high cortisol and low DHEA (see *The ABCs of Burning Body Fat*). This imbalanced state causes your body to burn more sugar and less fat as a fuel, which in turn causes you to store more fat. Accompanying low thyroid function is also common.

- **Reduced immunity.** Another result of hormone imbalance is reduced immunity. This makes you more vulnerable to any type of infection, from bacteria and viruses to yeast and fungal infections (i.e., candida). These infections are often treated with antibiotics or other drugs, rather than seeking out the cause of the reduced immunity, often due to some type of hormonal imbalance.

- **Diminished bone and muscle strength.** This can lead to fractures, injury and general weakness. Low estrogen and progesterone often cause the problem in women, and low testosterone causes these problems in men. But primary to these problems is usually an imbalance between cortisol and DHEA.

- **Amenorrhea.** The lack of a menstrual period is especially common in athletes and women under stress. Low DHEA, and low progesterone followed by low estrogen are common patterns of imbalance. Cortisol is almost always a primary hormone problem.

- **Menopausal symptoms.** This problem is usually due to a lack of adrenal-hormone production following diminished ovarian hormone output — estrogen and progesterone being the common culprits. High or low cortisol may be a primary factor.

- **Premenstrual syndrome (PMS).** Whether you've experienced it or been the target of those who are affected by it, you know what PMS is. While it's a problem often cited by comedians, it is a serious lifestyle issue and an indication of hormonal imbalance. This may be associated with reduced progesterone, high cortisol, low DHEA or, most likely, combinations of several hormone imbalances.

- **Reduced sexual function.** This is most often due to hormone imbalance, especially DHEA and testosterone. Restoring hormone balance typically results in a return of sexual desire and improved sexual function.

- **The stress cycle.** Hormone imbalance is the result of and further provokes additional stress, maintaining a vicious cycle. Once caught in this stress cycle, many healthy body functions, including brain function, begin to deteriorate. Quality of life is reduced as you age faster. Left unchecked, this could even lead to disease conditions.

- **Other conditions.** These include insomnia, depression, eating disorders and infertility. Insomnia occurs when cortisol is too high during the night. Depression is associated with a variety of hormone imbalances, as are eating disorders. Infertility may be associated with insulin excess, with secondary low levels of estrogen and progesterone.

The ABCs of Hormones

Your hormones are produced from the head down, mostly by glands throughout the body. But some hormones are also made in organs, such as the heart and intestines. Generally, the process starts in the brain in an area called the hypothalmus, which has close ties with the emotions and other parts of the nervous system. The hypothalmus produces certain hormones that affect the pituitary gland in the brain, which in turn sends the hormone ACTH (adrenocorticotropic hormone) down to the body where certain glands (i.e., the adrenals) are stimulated to produce other hormones. This example is referred to as the hypothalmic-pituitary-adrenal axis. Another important relationship exists as the hypothalmic-pituitary-ovarian axis. Just to give you an idea of how complex things can get, the hormones in each of these mechanisms can affect the other hormone mechanisms, and virtually any other hormone can react to any other hormone.

Cortisol is one of the key hormones for two reasons. First, it increases with any type of stress — physical, chemical or mental. This also includes anaerobic training (higher-intensity workouts, weight-lifting and competition). Second, if cortisol is increased too much, all other hormones on the chart are reduced. As a result, the most common situation of hormonal imbalance is high cortisol, accompanied by low DHEA, testosterone, progesterone and estrogen. Other patterns of imbalance are also possible. In cases of long-term stress, cortisol levels can become very low.

When the common pattern of excess cortisol and reduced DHEA occurs, an anabolic/catabolic imbalance also may follow. The correct balance of anabolic and catabolic activity is necessary in order to reach athletic potential and optimal health without overtraining. As you train and race, you must rebuild your body — the muscles especially, but also bones, blood vessels, heart and immune system. This is referred to as being in an anabolic state. When your body is breaking down, it is referred to as a catabolic state. This tearing-down process takes place as part of the training cycle. However, too much catabolic activity leads to injury, ill health and reduced performance, a condition I call the overtraining syndrome. In addition to high cortisol and low DHEA, low testosterone in both men and women is associated with an anabolic/catabolic imbalance.

Insulin also is often high when there is an imbalance, and only when the person is diabetic will it potentially be at very low levels (or there will be no production at all). In many diabetics, however, there is enough insulin produced but it can't be utilized due to insulin resistance by the cells (insulin is not recognized and therefore not functional).

When hormone imbalance occurs, it can have a dramatic and sometimes devastating effect on your health and fitness. One of the first problems is a reduction in performance — whether in your day-to-day life, work, or athleticism. This is not limited to physical performance, as mental performance also can be adversely affected, with symptoms including poor memory, reduced concentration and depression.

It's important to note that most of these hormones (the exception being insulin) are manufactured from cholesterol. And, it's been shown that a low-fat diet results in lower levels of some of these hormones (except insulin, which may increase with a low-fat diet).

Causes of stress and the remedies can vary significantly, as it is a very individual problem. Evaluating your physical stress is a good start. Are your training shoes in good shape? Do you slouch when sitting?

One remedy, as discussed above, is to look at your stress, eliminate those that can be disposed of, and if possible modify as many of the others as possible. One of the items easily modified is training. This is the reason why cutting down on workouts in time and intensity often improves performance. By lowering your stress levels the adrenal glands can "catch up" and your health and fitness improves.

Mental tension about anything, or everything, is counterproductive for the adrenal glands. Meditation, whether done formally in a quiet location, or informally when training by yourself, is often very helpful.

Other remedies can include natural substances, such as vitamins, minerals, phytonutrients, foods and even natural hormones that nature provides. Occasionally, your doctor may need to give you a natural hormone that can only be obtained through a prescription, or in some cases, a synthetic prescription hormone. More information on this subject is available in *Eating for Endurance* and *The ABCs of Hormonal Stress*.

Chemically, various nutrients are sometimes required when there is excess stress since the adrenals utilize these to function. Vitamins B6, C and pantothenic acid, and the mineral zinc, are common examples. An overconsumption of refined sugar or large amounts of caffeine are frequent excesses which can add burden to the adrenal glands.

10

Warming Up and Cooling Down

When the topic of warming up is mentioned, most people think of stretching. While stretching is important for those who participate in certain sports like track and field, gymnastics and ballet, it is much less significant, and too often harmful, for those participating in endurance sports.

For endurance athletes, properly warming up and cooling down is more important than stretching. A warm-up prepares the body for activity and is an integral part of every training session and competition. A good warm-up reduces the muscle soreness associated with the early stages of an exercise program, decreases the risk of injury and may be the most important "therapeutic" aspect of exercise. On the other hand, eliminating a warm-up can result in an abnormal electrocardiogram, myocardial ischemia, and poor blood pressure response following exercise, even in healthy, fit individuals.

Warming up refers to preparation of the body for training. The warming occurs partly from an increase in blood circulation. With the onset of your workout, the muscles quickly require much more oxygen and other nutrients, and have waste products that must be removed. This request by the muscles is accomplished by an increase in blood circulation. As discussed earlier, the aerobic muscles are well endowed with blood vessels, and most of the circulation is directed there.

If the muscles are receiving more blood, where does it come from? The answer to this question is the most important and significant aspect of warming up.

At rest, your body devotes much of its circulation to the organs and glands — the liver, adrenals, brain and spinal cord, etc. From a standpoint of blood circulation, this resting state is just the opposite of working out.

When you begin your workout, and the muscles require more circulation, more than half of the blood flow going to the organs and glands gets detoured into the working muscles. During an anaerobic workout, up to 80 percent of the blood is shifted to the muscles. While this satisfies the muscle's demands, the organs and glands suddenly may lack the circulation necessary for optimal function. In many ways, this is a major stress to the organs and glands when the shift occurs too quickly.

The remedy — the way to satisfy the whole body — has to do with timing. If the organs and glands slowly relinquish their circulation at the same time the blood flow to the muscles is gradually increased, the potential stress is minimized.

When this happens, the neurological, metabolic and muscular body is optimally prepared for the remaining part of the workout. One of the significant benefits of an active warm-up is the elevation of body temperature, which serves a number of purposes, including:

- Increased blood flow to working muscles.

- Greater mechanical efficiency.

- Release of circulating fatty acids useful for energy in aerobic muscle fibers and vital capacity.

- Increased range of motion (ROM).

In order to accomplish this, the muscle action should begin very easily and gradually build up. Often, athletes start off a workout with too much intensity, which quickly shifts the blood flow from organs and glands, potentially causing stress.

A heart monitor is a very helpful tool for warming up. Let's say you want to go for an aerobic workout, and your max aerobic heart rate is 140 (with a range of 130-140). As you step out the door you notice your heart rate is 60. A proper warm-up would dictate that you reach your 140 heart rate only after about 15 minutes for most workouts. Slowly raise your heart rate from the 60s to the 70s, 80s, etc. until you reach the 130-140 range after 15 minutes. For training lasting more than about 90 minutes, the warm up should be extended — perhaps to about 20 minutes or more.

Ideally, your warm up should be tailored to your body's needs. Once you get used to warming up properly, you may notice your body requiring more warm-up time, even for a short workout. If this is the case, heed your body's signal and extend your warm-up time. Never assume, however, that you need less than a 15-minute warm-up.

Cooling Down

Once you're turned on your body and provided it with a workout, the final stage is recovery. This is initiated with a cool-down.

The cool-down is just the opposite of a warm-up; slowly allow the heart rate to descend. While you will not reach your starting heart rate, you may come within 10 or 20 beats of it. For example, if you head out the door at a heart rate of 60, a proper cool down may bring you back to 70-80.

This slow descent in intensity prevents physical and chemical stress, especially within the cardiovascular system and the muscle fibers.

For most workouts, spend about 15 minutes cooling down. For longer workouts, such as 4 or more hours, increase this time to at least 20-30 minutes.

The following graphs depict proper and improper ways of warming up. The main benefit of the cool down is it begins the process of recovery from the workout by assuring more blood flow is returned to the organs and glands.

The first graph plots heart rate and time, and indicates the proper warm-up and cool-down. The next graph illustrates the incorrect way to warm up and cool down. In this case, the heart rate jumps immediately to the training level. At the end of the workout, the heart rate descends too quickly.

The time spent warming up and cooling down is part of your total workout — a very important portion. So, if you plan on a one-hour aerobic run, you will spend 15 minutes warming up, 15 cooling down, and a half hour in your aerobic training zone.

Let me repeat what was noted above: the warm-up prepares your body for the workout, and the cool-down initiates the recovery process.

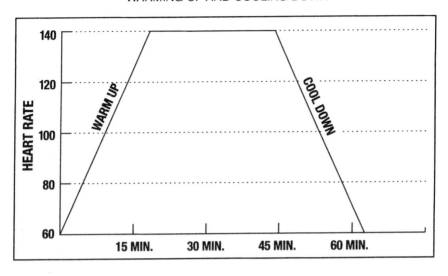

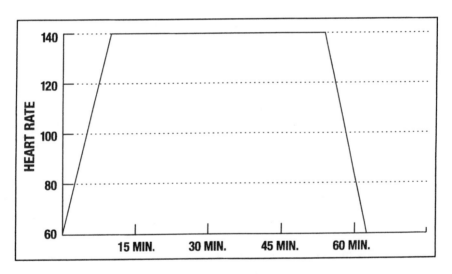

Don't be fooled into thinking that because you don't feel like you're getting much of a workout that the warm-up and cool-down doesn't count as part of it. Tremendous health benefits are obtained through these aspects of your program. An overtrained athlete often has arrived in that state because of a lack of warming up and cooling down. Nagging injuries sometimes disappear when a long enough warm-up precedes the workout. Even racing is improved when the body is properly warmed.

Stretching vs. Flexibility

Many athletes associate stretching with warming up. But stretching does not accomplish what a real warm-up does. Many also think stretching will prevent injury and improve performance. Not only is this not true, but often, just the opposite can occur.

It's very important, however, that athletes increase their flexibility. This can be done with a proper warm-up. Even patients with arthritis can improve flexibility with an aerobic warm-up, as much as by stretching.

There are two basic types of stretching, referred to as static and ballistic. Static stretching is a very slow, deliberate movement, where you lightly stretch a muscle and hold it statically (unchanged) for 10-30 seconds. When properly done, this activity promotes relaxation of the muscle being stretched. Optimal static stretching requires that each muscle group be sequentially repeated three to four times. It also demands that the activity be done slowly and not rushed.

There are two types of static stretching. Of these, active is much more safe than passive. Active stretching is accomplished by contracting the antagonist muscle (the one opposite the muscle you're stretching). For example, to actively stretch the hamstring muscles, the quadriceps are contracted.

Passive stretching uses gravity or force by another body part or person to move a body segment to the end of its range of motion or beyond — the reason this form of stretching can so easily cause injury.

The second basic type of stretching is called ballistic. This is a "bouncing" method and is the most common type of stretching done by athletes and beginners. It makes use of the body's momentum to repeatedly stretch a joint position to or beyond the extreme ranges of motion. Because this method is more rapid than static stretching, it activates the stretch reflex, which increases tension in the muscle, rather than relaxation. This can result in micro-tearing of muscle fibers with resultant injury.

Ballistic stretching is the type most say they don't do, but most really employ. That's because most athletes are in a hurry when stretching before or after training. Pre-race tension tends to make one stretch in a more stressful and quick mode, forcing you to stretch more ballistically.

Flexibility refers to the relative range of motion allowed at a joint. This is related to the tension in the muscles that move or restrict the joint.

The risk of injury is increased when:

- Joint flexibility is increased too much.

- Joint flexibility is greatly diminished.

- An imbalance in joint flexibility exists between left and right, or front and back, sides of the body.

A study of U.S. Army recruits found that the least flexible and the most flexible were more than twice as likely to get injured compared to those whose joints had moderate flexibility.

Endurance athletes who do stretch generally are more injured than those who don't stretch. That has not only been my observation over nearly 20 years of treating athletes, but the opinion and observation of many other professionals. In addition, scientific studies support these observations.

One common example used to show the increased injury rate in stretchers versus non-stretchers is the hamstring muscles. It is both the most frequently injured muscle group, and the most stretched.

Halbertsma, in a study of men and women 20-38 years of age with tight/stiff hamstrings, states that "stretching exercises do not make short hamstrings any longer or less stiff."

Richard Dominguez, M.D., an orthopedic surgeon at Loyola University Medical Center and author of *Total Body Training* (Charles Scribner's Sons, 1982) and *The Complete Book of Sports Medicine* (Encore Editions, 1979) also disapproves of stretching. "Flexibility should not be a goal in itself, but the result of . . . training. Strengthening the muscles around a joint naturally increases flexibility. If you can bend a joint beyond your ability to control it with muscle strength, you risk either tearing the muscles, tendons or ligaments that support the joint, or damaging the joint through abnormal pressure on it."

Among the specific stretches Dominguez says are most damaging are the yoga plow, hurdler's stretch, toe touching, and the stiff leg raise.

The types of injury created by stretching may be in the muscle itself, the tendon and ligament associated with that muscle, or even the joint controlled by that muscle.

Exercise repetition from swimming, biking, running and other endurance sports results in an already slight overstretched state. The chemical reaction to stretching, whether from a normal workout or the act of stretching, increases the production of chemicals called prostaglandins, which increases inflammation. Adding more stretching only increases the potential for more inflammation.

Many athletes stretch thinking it will help performance. But studies show this is not the case. Static stretching not only does not improve athletic performance, but may actually hinder it.

For those who require a wider range of motion, stretching may be necessary. But these athletes include dancers, sprinters and gymnasts, and not endurance athletes.

Case History

Randy began his morning with 10 minutes of stretching. Then the first 15 minutes of his workout was spent climbing hills from his house in the valley. When he first used a heart monitor, his rate surged to 180 within five minutes. But he could not imagine how any of that was related to his low back pain. By performing manual muscle testing, we discovered that Randy's hamstring muscles were overstretched and weak, not helping to support his lower back. Therefore the first recommendation was to stop stretching his already overstretched hamstrings. Within a couple of weeks the lower back improved. This was followed by the difficult task of adjusting the morning ride to avoid the hills. The only solution was for Randy to ride on his rollers for about 15 minutes before going out the door, then riding very slowly until getting past the hills. When he was able to accomplish this, his chronic asthma also disappeared.

Yoga and other "whole-body" flexibility activities are very different from stretching as I've described it above. When properly done using a very slow, deliberate and easy motion, whole-body flexibility activities are healthy, safe and very effective. Applied kinesiologist Sam Yanuck describes this well: "In all my years of martial training, I've learned to stretch like animals. They gently stretch the whole body at once, in a mild way, from the tip of the toes to the top of the head and to the ends of the fingers."

11

Aerobic Training

By far, the most important aspect of training for endurance is developing the entire aerobic system. This includes good circulation, slow-twitch muscle fiber development and the ability to burn large amounts of fat for energy. Diminishing performance, injury and ill health almost always stem from a lack of aerobic function.

In this chapter, I want to discuss several important aspects of aerobic training. These include building an aerobic base, aerobic intervals, downhill or neurological workouts, aerobic speed and walking.

The first step in producing a highly efficient aerobic system is building a large, solid aerobic base. This phase of your training is a period of time when all your workouts are aerobic. Specifically this means at or below your maximum aerobic heart rate determined by the 180 Formula. It means every workout is aerobic. That includes the Sunday group ride, Saturday's hilly run in the park and any other workouts where you're heavily influenced by other athletes or the terrain.

In addition, an aerobic base period also is void of weight-lifting, since this is also an anaerobic workout. This is the part of training where discipline, dedication and hard work are important. Most athletes think these three mental attributes are related to toughing it out, grunting and training in pain. But it's sometimes harder than that. Training properly during the aerobic phase, for many athletes, is the most difficult part of the program. It's the ability to go slow, despite what other athletes are doing and saying.

Many athletes complain initially about the slowness of the pace. They say it's too easy. This relatively slow pace is normal, especially if you have not built a good aerobic base. If you don't feel like you've done much after an aerobic workout, you're on target.

For other athletes, those who have successfully built a good aerobic base, the aerobic pace is not always excessively easy. But you don't progress to that level overnight, and success means starting at the right point. For many, this means starting slowly.

Although your aerobic training will feel too easy and you'll wonder if you're benefiting, your pace will quicken in time. This may happen in a matter of weeks depending on many factors, the main one being stress. For many, some stress is in the form of anaerobic work, for others it's job stress, and still for some a combination of stresses. Sometimes it's just "life's stress."

It's easy to measure your progress, and very important that you do. The MAF Test can guide you through your base. If you're really building properly, you'll see your pace improve. But if you're knowingly or unknowingly sneaking in some anaerobic work, you risk slowing or stopping the base-building process.

How does anaerobic work interfere with building an aerobic base? Before explaining that, here's the bottom line: Anaerobic work can dramatically interfere with aerobic and endurance development. The MAF Test, for example, shows a quicker plateau often followed by regression. In some athletes, it only takes one anaerobic workout or race per week during the aerobic base period to inhibit aerobic development. In others, daily stress levels, which chemically mimic anaerobic activity, are enough to inhibit aerobic progress. And often, nutritional and dietary problems limit base-building.

There may be several reasons why anaerobic workouts at the wrong time can inhibit aerobic base-building:

- Anaerobic training can decrease the number of aerobic muscle fibers, sometimes significantly. This can happen in just a few short weeks of improper training.

89

- The lactic acid produced during anaerobic training may inhibit the aerobic muscle enzymes which are necessary for aerobic metabolism.

- Anaerobic training raises your respiratory quotient. This means your percentage of energy derived from sugar increases and fat-burning decreases. In time, this may force more anaerobic metabolism and less aerobic function.

- Stress also has a physiologic response in the body, and can inhibit the aerobic system. Stress is nearly synonymous with anaerobic training. Excess stress raises cortisol levels, which ultimately increases insulin levels, inhibiting fat-burning and increasing sugar usage. This promotes anaerobic metabolism and inhibits aerobic activity.

- Nutrition and diet can also prevent you from building a good aerobic base. Too much dietary carbohydrate, including sweets, or too little essential fat in the diet can inhibit the aerobic system. In both instances, fat-burning is inhibited (see *Eating for Endurance*).

When all the endurance ingredients are mixed properly, the aerobic base develops and your pace increases as shown by your MAF Test. As your workout pace increases, you develop more aerobic speed.

Aerobic speed means you're able to swim, bike, run, skate or ski at a faster pace with the same effort. You've successfully developed your metabolism so you convert more fat to energy. In addition to possessing more aerobic speed, your adrenal function can improve as well, enabling you to better handle stress, store less fat, stabilize blood sugar and become less vulnerable to injury.

As your aerobic speed increases, so does your performance. That's because you're able to race at a faster pace with the same effort as measured by heart rate. In a real sense, increased aerobic speed equates to faster anaerobic speed.

While building your aerobic base, there is a technique which can develop more speed without becoming anaerobic. It's called a downhill or neurological workout. This activity, as the name implies, involves going downhill to relieve some of the gravity stress. In this way you can increase your turnover while keeping your heart rate within your aerobic zone. In order to maintain your aerobic maximum heart rate, you will have to increase your effort, and this results in running, biking, skating, etc. at a much faster rate.

For example, at a heart rate of 145, if you can run at a 7:45 pace on flat ground, then running down a hill at the same heart rate will force you to run much faster, perhaps at a 6:50 pace.

Using a long downhill that's not too steep, you can train your nervous system to turn the legs over much more quickly than would ordinarily occur during a run on a flat course. If you have a long steady downhill that takes you 10 or 15 minutes, or longer, to complete, you can derive great benefits, including quicker turnover with your legs, without the stress of an anaerobic workout.

Be sure the downhill is not too steep a grade, which may force you to overstride. Even on the right grade, your stride length should be about the same as if you were on level ground. If the downhill run takes 15 minutes, you can do "downhill repeats," slowly going back up the hill to start your course again. If you're lucky enough to find an easy downhill that takes you a longer time, that's great.

I often suggest one or two downhill workouts per week, not on consecutive days, during the base period. This workout can last 45 minutes to an hour and a half, including warm-up and cool-down. Because it's all aerobic, when you're done it will feel much like any other aerobic workout despite the quick pace. These workouts will also help you develop more aerobic speed because of the effect on the nervous system.

Once you have achieved a high level of aerobic speed, it may be difficult or impossible for you to reach your aerobic maximum heart rate, depending on the event. This is most true in the water, and cycling, skating or skiing on flat terrain.

At this stage of your development, you may be ready to add aerobic intervals to your program. Aerobic intervals enable you to train at your maximum aerobic heart for short periods despite the difficulty in maintaining that level of activity. This is usually reserved for the lower gravity events like swimming, but cyclists, skaters and skiers often improve to that point.

You'll know when you're ready for aerobic intervals; riding or swimming at your maximum aerobic heart rate will be physically very difficult because the pace is too fast. It is just the opposite of what you feel when first starting this program, where the pace may be too slow.

Since you won't be able to maintain your maximum aerobic heart rate for the whole workout, you can perform a short interval at that level, then slow down for a period of time, then go back to the maximum aerobic level.

Below is an actual example of a cyclist's aerobic interval workout. His max aerobic heart rate is 150, and the total workout time is 90 minutes:

- A 20 minute warm up followed by, a 10-minute segment consisting of 5 minutes at 150 heart rate, and 5 minutes at 125 heart rate.

- This 10-minute segment is repeated five times (totaling 50 minutes).

- A 20-minute cool-down.

With all the different aspects of aerobic base-building mentioned in this chapter — aerobic speed, downhill workouts and aerobic intervals — I have emphasized the importance of raising the heart rate to your maximum aerobic level. But what if you don't feel like working out with that high a heart rate on a given day? Will you still derive aerobic benefits?

The answer is yes — you will still receive aerobic benefits even if your heart rate is not at your maximum aerobic level. You actually burn a higher percentage of fat during this type of workout, and incorporate aerobic muscle fibers you may otherwise not use.

I have observed many athletes who initially did not wish to be competitive, but derived great aerobic benefits by training at lower aerobic levels — below their aerobic range. Adding more intense aerobic work onto that type of base often produces a great endurance athlete. Because of this, I often encourage competitors at certain times of the year to have "easy" days where the heart rate never reaches the max aerobic level.

Often, especially during the racing season, training every other day at these easy levels helps speed recovery, and at the same time builds the small aerobic muscle fibers important for aerobic function. This can have a very positive effect on racing because these muscle fibers help break down lactic acid, improve circulation and burn fat for energy.

In addition, this technique is most helpful preceding a long race like the Ironman or a stage race lasting several days. During the tapering process, which I recommend beginning about two to four weeks before the race, train at least every other day below your maximum aerobic level.

Training this way at key points during the season can also help maintain your high aerobic and anaerobic levels previously developed, while training less.

An even better approach to building the small aerobic muscles is to walk regularly as a workout. Whether you're a cyclist, swimmer, runner or skater, walking once or twice a week can be very helpful. This is true for everyone, from the rookie competitor to the greatest endurance athlete. Spend at least an hour on your walk, more if you wish. In the beginning, an hour will seem like a long time. Eventually, an hour will seem too short and you may want to spend more time. You won't have too much success finding a training partner, but you may be better going it alone.

The walking workout can be done anytime in your schedule. It works especially well the day before a race. Walking is not only physiologically beneficial, but also can help mentally. Use it as a meditation, to help you focus on your body and its health.

Whatever your particular style of training or workout schedule, the most important aspect is your aerobic base. Within that base, and the way to fine-tune it, are specific techniques that increase your aerobic speed; they include downhill workouts, aerobic intervals and walking. In addition, performing the MAF Test helps qualify your overall training. With so much variation, building an aerobic base should be an interesting and exciting adventure.

Case History

John was in his fourth year of building a winter base, and his MAF was 7:10, down from 9:45 when he first began. His schedule is as follows:

Monday: 6 a.m. — easy 45-minute swim.
5:30 p.m. — easy 45-minute run.

Tuesday: 6 a.m. — one-hour swim at max heart rate.
5 p.m. — two-hour bike (aerobic intervals).

Wednesday: 6 a.m. — 90-minute run at max heart rate.

Thursday: 6 a.m. — one-hour swim at max heart rate.

Friday: 6 a.m. — one-hour downhill run.

Saturday: 8 a.m. — three-hour bike.
4:30 p.m. — easy 45-minute swim.

Sunday: 8 a.m. — two-hour bike (aerobic intervals), followed by a one-hour run.

John also enters one or two races (usually 10K) during the winter months, often running a personal best.

12

Anaerobic Training

Once you have built sufficient aerobic function, your body may be ready to add anaerobic work. I say "may" because many endurance athletes can often bypass this part of training and rely instead on racing to get all the anaerobic stimulation necessary.

An important question to answer about anaerobic workouts is, when should you begin them? One answer I frequently give is, if in doubt about when to start, wait. Build more base.

The main purpose of anaerobic training is to build the fast-twitch muscle fibers, thereby increasing anaerobic speed. For endurance athletes, maximum benefits can be achieved easily, and in as short a time as three to four weeks. Research has shown that for some people indicators of overtraining begin to show up as early as this same time frame.

Anaerobic workouts can be treacherous domain. This risky training is frequently the cause of injuries, fatigue and poor performance.

Still, some athletes are able to benefit from anaerobic work if properly done. If this is your situation, I have two recommendations:

- Keep it simple.

- Keep it short.

Keep It Simple
By keeping it simple, I am referring to the specific types of workouts in each sport. Some anaerobic-interval workouts have become so compli-

cated that you almost need a computer and an engineering degree to follow them.

After many years of assigning hundreds of styles of anaerobic intervals in many sports, I have concluded without a doubt that all of these different methods result in the same or very similar benefits when it comes to endurance athletes. Whether a runner does 400-meter repeats or hill repeats, step-ups or fartlek, the anaerobic stimulation will provide very similar if not identical results for racing. If the swimmer does varying distance intervals with any number of specific patterns offered by the many successful coaches in the sport, he or she will obtain the same or identical benefits for endurance races.

The most significant concern with anaerobic workouts is that they don't overstress the athlete. Unfortunately, this is most often the case. Dan is a typical example.

Case History

Dan had just completed a successful winter aerobic base period and was ready for spring track work. His favorite race distance was 10K, and this year his goal was to break 40 minutes. He began his track sessions with quarter-mile repeats at 75 seconds each, with a quarter-mile jog in between. When race time came, his times were only a few seconds faster than the previous year. What's worse, his times got slower as the season wore on and he never came close to breaking 40 minutes.

Why was Dan doing his intervals so fast? He has not yet broken 40 minutes for 10K, so his interval pace of 75 second quarters is far beyond his racing ability. He would produce much less stress and get the same benefit if his quarters were 90 seconds. This would provide a much bigger net gain.

If we looked at Dan's heart rate, we'd get a better idea of how stressful his workout was. Running a quarter-mile in 75 seconds brought Dan's heart rate to about 180. At 35 years of age, this is very close to his maximum heart rate. Running the same quarter mile at 90 seconds would bring his heart rate to about 170, closer to 90 percent of his max heart rate. This represents a more efficient training heart rate for an anaerobic workout.

The first simple suggestion for anaerobic work is that your heart rate not exceed 90 percent of its maximum heart rate, regardless of the type of workout. For example, if you're doing intervals on a track, use the heart rate as your primary guide, along with your time. On a bike, keep an eye on your heart rate more than the other riders.

My favorite recommendation for anaerobic workouts is fartlek. In addition to muscular, metabolic and neurological benefits, it also incorporates an important mental aspect of training; specifically, it forces you to become more aware of your body and its needs. For many, this style is a relief from the burden of the clock. In time, you may be able to do the whole workout by intuition and be relieved of the need to even look at your heart rate.

Keep It Short

If the duration of anaerobic workouts is excessive, it can also contribute to overtraining and ill health. So the second principle is keep it short. This relates to both the time of each workout, and the number of weeks these workouts are maintained.

Your neurological, metabolic and muscular body has a limit on what it can gain from a given individual anaerobic workout. And I do mean limit: 45 minutes for high-stress activity such as running, 60 to 90 minutes for other activities like cycling, skating and swimming. This is, however, sufficient time to get substantial benefits. And remember, these times include your warm up and cool down. So after this workout, don't expect to come home ready to collapse; it's not necessary.

How long should you continue doing the anaerobic part of your schedule? That depends on a number of factors. The biggest is stress — specifically, how much stress do you have in other areas of your life? Since stress and anaerobic work create similar metabolic states, the more stress you have the less anaerobic work you should do.

Another important factor is time. How much time do you have, especially for recovery? It takes longer to recover from anaerobic sessions, and if your days and evenings are generally busy with other commitments, you may not have the luxury of doing much anaerobic work.

The best way to answer the question of how long you should continue anaerobic work is by performing the MAF Test. If you see a slowing of your pace at any time during your anaerobic training phase, it's time to stop and return to aerobic base training. A worsening of your MAF Test would indicate you've done too much anaerobic work. As many athletes find, only a few short weeks of anaerobic training is all that's required.

For most endurance athletes, the maximum time for anaerobic work is about eight weeks. This is the maximum, and more of an exception. For the average endurance athlete who works a 40-hour per week job, especially if he or she has a family, five weeks may be possible. Most athletes can obtain maximum anaerobic benefits after three to four weeks. But for many, no anaerobic training is best.

By now, you're asking yourself the customary question; "How will I get fast if I don't train fast?" Let me emphasize as I did earlier, and assure you that endurance races are 95-99 percent aerobic. You will increase your race speed by getting more efficient through aerobic training.

Going through a yearly schedule without anaerobic work is a dramatic break from tradition. But once you've done it, and see the positive results, you'll have no trouble creating a new tradition.

Actually, you are performing some anaerobic work when you're racing. For many athletes, that's just enough hard input to keep the body balanced and working well.

Consider triathlete Mike Pigg's 1994 season — one of his best. He won most of his races and finished high up in most of the rest. He did not do any anaerobic work until mid-September, when most of his races were completed.

When anaerobic training is included in your schedule, there are a few basic rules to follow:

- Including races, do not exceed two to three anaerobic workouts per week.

- For many athletes, one anaerobic workout per week is sufficient.

- Most athletes will reach maximum anaerobic benefits after three or four weeks of anaerobic work.

- Workouts the day before and after an anaerobic workout should be easy ones; never perform anaerobic workouts on two consecutive days.

- Try to mimic your race environment during anaerobic workouts. This includes running on the road, cycling with a group, or swimming open water.

- Focus on relaxation and breathing to increase your mechanical efficiency. If you're uptight and stressed, do an easy workout and try again the next day.

- Try to do your anaerobic workout in the morning, or about the same time as the start of your races.

- Be sure to warm up and cool down sufficiently.

- Treat your anaerobic workout mentally and physically as if it were a race.

- Be sure to eat and drink enough fluid before and after your workout.

Case History
In the case of John, portrayed at the end of the last chapter, his anaerobic schedule typically looks like this:

Monday: 6 a.m. — Easy 45-minute swim.
5:30 p.m. — Easy 45-minute run.

Tuesday: 6 a.m. — One-hour swim at max aerobic heart rate.
5 p.m. — Two-hour bike: time trial.

Wednesday: 6 a.m. — 90-minute run at max aerobic heart rate.

Thursday: 6 a.m. — One-hour swim at max aerobic heart rate.

Friday: 6 a.m. — One-hour fartlek run (anaerobic).
Saturday: 8 a.m. — Three-hour bike. 4:30 p.m. — Easy 45-minute swim.

Sunday: 8 a.m. — Two-hour bike (aerobic intervals), followed by easy one-hour run.

John follows this schedule for about four weeks, after which he begins his racing season.

A Word about Weights

Weight-lifting is anaerobic, whether you're lifting low weight and using high repetition, or the reverse. But don't expect to see your heart rate increase beyond your maximum aerobic level during a weight session. In most people, the muscle which you are working fatigues before the heart rate reaches its peak level. Since you stop lifting at that point, your heart rate never reaches its highest level. So using the heart rate to judge whether your weight workout is anaerobic is not accurate. The bottom line: Weight-lifting is anaerobic. So treat it that way in relation to your weekly schedule.

Weight-lifting's place in endurance sports is a controversial subject when discussed by athletes, coaches and physiologists. For most endurance athletes, I don't think the need exists, nor do I think it is an effective use of time.

Weight workouts help the muscle, or group of muscles, to be stronger during the specific action trained during the workout. Most often, that action does not imitate the exact action during your endurance race. The result is little to no improvement in power during competition.

Weight-lifting uses up a lot of energy during training, and builds muscle bulk. This added mass induces weight gain, sometimes significantly, which can be a negative factor during competition. In addition, in order to maintain the benefits of weight-lifting, you must continue this activity throughout the year, if only once or twice weekly. Otherwise, most if not all of your gains will be lost.

Some feel the added muscle gained during lifting will protect them from injury. But it's the aerobic muscle fibers which perform this work much more than the anaerobic fibers built during weight training.

In addition, the average endurance athlete already has a tough schedule: training, working, family or home responsibilities, and perhaps other obligations. Finding time for another workout — often two or three — adds stress to an often overbusy week.

If your schedule permits two or three added workouts per week, and you have built as good an aerobic base as possible, you may consider weights as an added workout. In addition, if you have lost muscle mass, due to reduced training for example, or injury, then weight-lifting can serve a valuable purpose. Or, if you're 30 or 40 years old or older, and you're just starting to work out, adding weight after your first good aerobic base may benefit you.

Think of all anaerobic training, including weights, as an investment. It's a high risk with a small return. Would you spend money on such a scheme? In addition, fitting these workouts into your schedule — without sacrificing aerobic benefits — may be adding yet another stress to your week. Fortunately, most endurance athletes can obtain all the anaerobic stimulation necessary from racing. And racing after building a good aerobic base results in great performances.

13

Training Schedules for Age-Group Athletes

L earning how to train for both health and fitness involves a number of factors — experience, technique, intuition, and some basic knowledge about the body. There are also some fundamental considerations about piecing together your training schedule, considering you may have an even busier job with the rest of your life's chores. By far the most important consideration is this:

First, understand the primary rules of training — warming up, cooling down, monitoring your heart rate, etc. — and successfully apply them. Then, your day-to-day schedule becomes a secondary feature — exactly how many minutes per day you train is no longer the main focus. It will fall into place on its own.

Perhaps a better title for this chapter is "Less is More." Meaning that for the average athlete with many other responsibilities, less training usually produces better athletic performances than trying to accumulate many miles and hours of training.

The majority of the athletes I have worked with in my career, like most of the readers of this book, are not professionals. If you work a full-time job, perhaps have a family, a house and other responsibilities, you can still train and perform at very high levels. But don't expect to be able to put in the same amount of time and miles as professional athletes. Nor do you need to for success. As a matter of fact, many professionals put in much less time training than you think.

Most of the time, I find that diminishing the total training hours per week allows for more recovery and less stress. This helps the aerobic system build itself much more efficiently. When race season comes, you're more refreshed and ready to race.

Case History

Carla was a back-of-the-pack triathlete with hopes of improving her performances. But after her fourth year of diminishing returns, she sought help with her schedule. After reading one of my earlier books, she strictly followed the program, except for one thing — her workout schedule averaged 18 hours per week. Unfortunately, Carla really didn't have the time for that amount of training, but she tried to squeeze in the workouts. She worked part time and had a family that included two young children.

In mid-November, I recommending she cut her schedule to about 12 hours per week. It was also the only change necessary. Carla was doing everything else right. By the end of next summer's racing season, eight out of nine races were personal bests. Carla also placed in the top five of her age group in half of those events.

For many years, scientists have known that there is a limit to how much an athlete can train before it adversely affects race performance.

The majority of your physical benefits received from training occur in the first 10 weeks of the season. The benefits obtained in this early phase, such as VO_2 max, can be maintained very easily with much less training. One study showed that maintaining VO_2 max could be accomplished by cutting training by two-thirds!

If you train regularly, year after year, your improvement will be slower through the later years compared to early on, but you can maintain that improvement with much less effort. Additional effort will not necessarily produce more improvements.

Classic scientific studies show no evidence that, for single-sport activities, multiple daily training sessions improve performance more than single daily sessions. Studies on swimmers demonstrated that heart rate and lactate levels, and performance times, were no different between two groups of athletes, one training twice daily and one with a single workout.

While many of these investigations are short-term, longer studies provide the same information regarding training volume. Research which examined swimmers over a five-year period showed those who swam 10,000 meters daily performed no differently than those who trained daily at half that distance.

Despite the evidence that less training offers more benefits, endurance athletes still overtrain too often. Part of the problem may be social. Our social trend in athletics today, especially in the United States, is still that of "no pain, no gain." This philosophy is asserted in advertising, magazine articles and schools, and has become a vicious cultural cycle. And, our very young athletes are exposed to this conviction long before they learn about being healthy and fit. In many cases, they learn about the latter after it's too late.

Learning about yourself will help determine an ideal schedule. This includes commitment, time allotment, goals, etc. Applying that information to your particular sport is the next step for success.

If you are training for a single sport, your schedule is usually easier than if you are a multisport athlete. Most of the time, you'll have one workout a day. The best time to do this is based more on your daily non-training schedule. When do you work? What other obligations exist? Many runners, for example, find a morning workout most suitable. Other sports have limits; swimmers usually have pool hours to consider, cyclists and skiers the weather. I frequently recommend single-sport athletes perform some other activity one to three times per week. This cross-training has a positive benefit, especially for the nervous system, as long as it is aerobic and fits into your schedule.

If you are a multisport athlete with two or more sports, you'll have a busier schedule. But this does not mean you have to perform each sport every day.

One luxury of being a professional is that your job is to train and race. You have most, if not all, of the day available to train — not that you'd work out all day. A pro triathlete, for example, may swim an hour in the morning, go for a two-hour bike ride mid-day, and run an hour in the late afternoon. But if you're an age-group athlete, this schedule usually won't work.

For those doing more than one sport, you don't have the luxury of working out in all your events each day. Nor is that required. However, many endurance athletes attempt this, sometimes no matter what the outcome.

Case History

Jay was stuck in an overtraining cycle for at least three years. He would train in each of his three events as many days as possible. He would run at 5 a.m., swim at noon and ride late in the day. The problem: Jay had his own business and worked from 7 a.m. until 9 p.m. He also had a family. Maintaining that schedule five days, with Tuesday and Thursday reserved for his long bike ride and run respectively, was quite a chore.

Jay would become exhausted regularly, and about every couple of months he'd have to take a week or two off completely. As he started feeling better, he would pick up his "normal" schedule again. I gave Jay my version of a normal program, explaining how he would race better and get more healthy. However, he could not understand how one could improve without the high-mileage weeks. I never saw Jay again in the office, but occasionally would meet him at a race, where year after year he showed no improvement.

If you're a multisport athlete and get at least three days a week of each activity, your schedule can be very effective. If you attempt to do otherwise, you risk overtraining. If possible, spread these workouts through the week so they are not on consecutive days. For example:

Swim: Monday, Wednesday, Saturday

Bike: Tuesday, Thursday, Saturday, Sunday

Run: Monday, Thursday, Sunday

For most athletes, the weekend can provide longer workouts. Perhaps a longer bike on Saturday and longer run Sunday. Or, you can combine two events and make one longer workout such as a two-hour bike followed by a 45-minute run. A favorite winter workout is a swim immediately followed by an hour of indoor biking on rollers or a trainer. These combined sessions provide not only a longer workout but help mimic race transitions, where your body has to adjust to the stress of changing from one event to another.

Notice the above schedule has nothing planned for Friday. This is an off day, something most athletes don't get enough of. If you feel better calling this a rest or recovery day, go right ahead. Sometimes the word "off" refers to not doing anything. But these days provide a most important part of the training formula:

Training = work + rest

I recommend at least one rest day per week to help with recovery. During the racing season, when you will more easily maintain your fitness level with less training but require more recovery, two rest days are even better. Off days are best taken going into a weekend, if that is your busiest training time or if there is a race. Another appropriate time is Monday, which is a day when a lot of your energy is needed for recovery. Or make Monday an easy day if Friday is your off day and the weekend includes a lot of training.

When planning rest days (and easy ones), consider your work stress too. If Mondays are always your busiest or hardest on the job, don't train that day.

Seasonal stress may also be a factor. If you're an accountant and your busiest time is tax season in the early spring, make that an easy training time too, and postpone your racing until early summer.

Another important time to take it easy is at the end of your training and racing year. For most northern hemisphere athletes this is November or December. At this time I recommend taking two to three weeks completely off, or more if you need it. While periods of rest are helpful for the body, a mental break is just as important. During this time just let your body do what it wants: Watch TV, go for hikes, paint your house, etc.

At this point, you may be looking for me to provide a training schedule. There is none that would prove ideal for all the readers of this book. Keeping in mind all the rules — from warming up to proper heart rate to cooling down — and fitting your workouts into your week where they won't stress anyone, you'll have no trouble formulating your own schedule. This is the same way I did it for athletes ranging from age-groupers to professionals when I was in practice.

14

Getting Ready to Compete

For most athletes, this is what it's all about — competition. Competing should not only be rewarding and fun, but also educational. Racing is the culmination of all your discipline, the end result of your labor. But for too many, it's a time of disappointment. For racing success, three important actions must be effectively executed: preparation, implementation and recovery. These factors should help you answer the question: Are you ready to race?

Preparation

There are two important aspects of preparation. The first is tapering, and the second is knowing when your body is ready to race.

Tapering is a period of diminished training. It enables your body to rest and recover from the training that hopefully has been successful. Even though you are working out much less, this period of reduced activity should not take away from your race performance, but rather enhance it by assuring you are well rested for race day. Remember, this taper period will enhance your performance.

The routines I have used for years, which are supported by the published research of others, indicate that at least two weeks — and sometimes as much as three or four weeks — of tapering is optimal for long events like a marathon, a cycling tour or an Ironman. Even for shorter events, a few days of tapering can make a significant difference in performance.

During the taper period, reduce your training by 50 to 80 percent, with less training as you get closer to race day. In addition, avoid all anaerobic training during the taper period. Downhill runs or spinning on your bike can help the nervous system maintain its turnover capability.

The scientific literature shows that during a taper period your muscle strength actually increases. In addition, no reduction in VO_2 max or MAF occurs.

In a study using runners, a 60 percent reduction in training for 15 to 21 days showed no loss in either endurance or VO_2 max.

Another benefit of tapering is that resting significantly improves leg power; improved arm strength in swimmers has also been noted in studies. Other benefits include lower lactate levels once competition begins.

Tapering must be differentiated from detraining, which is the complete cessation of working out. With no training, endurance is adversely affected after only two weeks.

The second aspect of preparation is knowing when your body is ready to race. You can determine this using three methods:

1. The first and most effective is through information obtained from your MAF Test.

2. The second and most common is by the calendar.

3. The third and most dangerous is because everyone else is doing it.

The MAF Test Analysis

The most effective way to determine the ideal time to start racing is to assess your body. This is best accomplished by the MAF Test.

Building your aerobic base is the most important aspect of training, and the most significant factor in racing. So before embarking on competition, allow your body to build as much aerobic function as possible. An improvement in your aerobic speed and a natural plateau may indicate you've reached your maximum aerobic benefits for that base period.

Can competition be successful having only trained aerobically for up to several months? The answer is not only "yes," but you can more often compete at your best following a good aerobic base period.

Recall that endurance events are 95 percent or more aerobic in nature. This much aerobic requirement for racing may be part of the reason for the results in a clinical study I did in the early to mid 1980s. I found more than 75 percent of the runners I trained over a four-year period raced personal bests in their spring races following a winter aerobic base. The key point of this survey was to show that a majority of runners could compete well without anaerobic training.

For many endurance athletes, the ideal approach is to build a big base, typically in the winter, and start competing in the spring. Let the racing satisfy any need for anaerobic stimulation. This keeps your training schedule more free of stress, allows for more competition, and further assures you don't overtrain.

Case History
Charlie was racing better each of the last six years. Now at age 36, and in a new age group, he decided to continue the same strategy that was successful. He built a good winter base by only training aerobically. In the spring, he would begin road racing and duathlons as his tune up for the summer triathlons. As the season progressed, so did his racing. And each year his times for the same races improved over the previous year.

The Calendar Method
Just because it's April (or whatever the month) doesn't mean you have to compete. Don't let the calendar dictate your training and racing patterns; it may not correlate with your body's readiness.

If you want to compete at a certain time of year, make sure you're prepared by allowing enough time to build an aerobic base.

If you compete too early in your training calendar, or too much throughout it, competition can frequently be a frustrating and depressing experience.

The Go-with-the-Flow Method
Unfortunately, too many athletes don't plan for competition. By following what the crowd does, they allow others to do that for them.

Be your own athlete. And plan your season well ahead of time.

Competition should also be more than a casual, social event you jump into because you've got little else to do on a Sunday.

Obviously, the best way to determine race readiness is through objective assessment, such as with the MAF Test. In addition, there are other factors to consider when beginning to make that transition from training to competition, as discussed below.

Resting Heart Rate

The resting heart rate is one of the standby traditional biofeedback readings used for decades to help assess fitness. In the course of training, the resting heart rate normally lowers, the result of increased cardiac efficiency. If you have a cold or other stress looming over you, your resting heart rate increases a few or more beats reflecting the stress. So, if your rate is down over the previous couple of months, it may indicate race readiness.

However, the resting heart rate is not meant to be used exclusively as an indicator for anything, as doing that can mislead you. A case in point is during the third stage of overtraining, when your resting rate may actually diminish, making it appear like you're doing well. Without other indicators, you can easily be misled.

Weight and Body Fat

Many athletes gain weight over the winter, due either to training less, eating the wrong foods, or both. As you get into better shape, that weight usually drops — although so many athletes have excess body fat. But what do the numbers on the scale really tell you?

Scale weight only tells you how many pounds you weigh, and not how much fat you have stored. Your lean body mass, mostly muscle, weighs much more than an equal volume of body fat. But fat takes up much more space than an equal weight of muscle. So, if you want to know about body fat, you need to measure it separately from your lean body mass.

Calipers, water tanks and electronic gadgets may provide you with fairly accurate information about your body-fat percentage. But, since fat takes up space and when you lose it you get thinner, it's easier and cheaper to just measure yourself with a tape measure, although you won't get a percentage. Also, maybe nearly as accurate measure is to just ask yourself if your pants that fit so well last October fit the same now.

The reason weight and body fat are indicators of your readiness to compete is two-fold; first, if your body weight is too high for your frame, it may make for a slower bike or run. That's due to more gravity stress, not to mention that more oxygen is required. But it does not mean the thinner you are the faster you'll be. Like everything else in life, the extremes are dangerous. If you're too thin and have lost too much lean body mass, you'll have less muscle for fat-burning which provides power for your events. And, if you have too little fat stored, your energy and hormonal systems — and protective padding — may be jeopardized.

The ideal, of course, is not to gain weight or excess body fat in the winter. So, if your program is effective, your weight and fat content will come down to "normal." If this is the case, it's likely you're ready to race.

Your Diary

We all have a story to tell. And if you keep a diary, part of your story is written in it. Like any story, you often have a good idea what may happen next. Is it time to compete? Read your diary.

Your diary might include everything from total time and heart rates of each workout, which course you took that day and how far you went. It may mention the weather, how you felt, along with your fears and dreams. Most importantly, your diary should include a chart of your MAF Tests. Neatly plot them out so a quick glance will give you the last few months of progress.

Looking back over the past few months in your diary, you can more objectively assess your progress. Look for consistency, and gradual increases in total time of each workout, indicating increased fitness.

Mental Readiness

As your diary pages fill, your training enjoyment should too. Note how you've felt along the way. For example, as your rides become longer, are they still playful? Is your long run leaving you with a more positive feeling about training? With this type of analysis, you'll more easily see your readiness — or disinclination — to compete.

Also, and even more subjective, is your intuition. As you derive benefits from training, you should not only get more fit, but more healthy.

And, as you build both your mental and physical health, you may find it easier to answer the question: "Am I ready to compete?"

Blood Chemistry

There is a chemical part of you that must also be ready to race. The minerals, proteins and enzymes which keep your aerobic engine running smoothly must be balanced before embarking on your season.

The best and easiest way to generally evaluate this component is a blood test. This can be done at a local laboratory, although you'll probably need an order from your doctor.

Individual labs may use different names for certain tests, but there are some essential items you'll want checked. In addition, your doctor may want additional tests per your specific needs. Below is a list of the basics:

- **Complete blood count (CBC) with indices.** This test measures the red blood cells, along with the hemoglobin, hematocrit and other associated factors. The white blood cells are also counted, with the percentage of each cell listed along with other factors.

- **Blood chemistry.** This common test is actually a measurement of many different elements in the blood. From sugar (glucose) to proteins (albumin and globulin), minerals (calcium, iron, sodium and potassium) to fats (total cholesterol with HDL and LDL, and triglycerides), and others. In all, there are at least 24 items this test measures (some labs do the shorter version, which I don't recommend). This test should be done in a fasting state — no food or liquid (other than water) for 12 hours. So the best time to get the test done is first thing in the morning after not eating all night.

- **Miscellaneous tests.** If the blood chemistry test above did not measure some key items, have them done in addition. For example, without your HDL and LDL cholesterol, the total cholesterol (measured above) provides much less information. In addition, the amount of iron in your blood (serum iron) and in your red blood cells (hemoglobin) is important, but so is the amount stored. This stored iron is called ferritin, and can be tested separately. If you have too little or too much ferritin, there could be problems; too little means there's not enough iron to take the place of what you lose (especially in sweat). Too much means that you could potentially increase unwanted free-radical chemicals which contribute to inflammation and other unpleasant conditions. (That's why taking iron supplements when it's not indicated can be dangerous.)

All these tests will require at least two tubes of blood to be drawn. This is not a significant loss during the training season; however, it's not recommend taking the test right before a race.

The so-called "normal" levels are spelled out on the test-result sheet. But laboratory "normals" are made, in part, from the average of the population, which gives you a very wide range. I prefer a more narrow range. Some doctors are aware of this factor and can help you with the right interpretation.

In general, however, blood tests are just a ruling-out process. They will tell you if there is any significant problem, such as anemia (iron deficiency) or hyperlipoproteinemia (high blood fats called triglycerides). But you could have a normal iron level and still have a nutritional need for iron, or normal triglycerides and still be storing them on your hips or in your arteries. Other comprehensive tests, including a good history, can give your doctor or other professional clues about these problems.

Pre-Race Practices

A component to competition is your pre-race routine — the habits you adopt the few days before your event.

It's Thursday, and you're getting ready for Sunday's race. Your habits over the next few days can make a dramatic difference in your race performance, and how well you recover.

Sometimes even subtle stresses can have significant effects on your race performance. Being aware of the most important ones, and making the appropriate adjustments, can help you have a more efficient and enjoyable race day.

Below are the most common mistakes I've seen athletes make in the days leading up to competition, and especially on race day.

- Perhaps the most common nutritional deficiency in athletes is water. Dehydration may increase with pre-race stress and especially hot weather. Athletes are too often dehydrated, with the problem more prevalent in the days before a race. The best way to remain hydrated is to drink small amounts of water — two to six ounces each time — throughout the day and evening, rather than a couple of high volume loads here and there. Carry a water bottle around with you during the days before your race, and on race morning.

- Stay out of the sun during the days prior to the race. You'll dehydrate more quickly in the sun. In addition — and even more important — the sun increases bodily stress which will have an adverse effect on your performance. So stay in the shade as much as possible. If you must go out in the sun, wear a hat and light clothing that covers you.

- Keep your workouts to a minimum, if at all, in both duration and intensity. The best rule regarding training the week of the race, especially the few days before, is "less is best." You'll receive no race benefits by training during these last few days. However, you want to keep loose, and too little activity can make you stiff and jittery. So, if you feel you want to work out, some short, easy bouts are ideal, but keep it to a minimum. And the day or two right before the race you should consider taking off completely, using walking to stay loose. (See "tapering" below for more specifics.)

- While most athletes ponder the power behind their muscles, they usually underestimate the power of the mind. But you can train it just like your muscles. You have control over some potentially stressful activity before you race, namely how you think. Negative thoughts about the race can and should be turned into a positive outlook with realistic aspirations. You are in charge of your mind, but traditions, past experiences (yours and those of other people) and other memories have major influences. So remember, you're there to have fun and perform the best you can.

115

- Continue to eat the same kinds of food you're used to — assuming you're on the right diet for your needs (see *Eating for Endurance*). Also try to stay on the same time schedule. Late-night dinners with foods and alcoholic beverages you don't usually consume can potentially be dangerous to your performance. Remember, the body doesn't like too much change.

- Follow the same race routine that has proven to work for you, assuming it's a healthy one. If you're not sure what works, pay more attention to your body. Don't just blindly copy what others do. Avoid trying new bike equipment, running shoes, drinks and food during the race. Experiment during training, not on race day.

- Warm up on race morning. Depending on the distance and race layout, you can walk or run. If the race is a triathlon, you may also want to swim for part of your warm-up. If you have an adequate aerobic base, a good warm-up should total at least about 20-30 minutes for most shorter races. If you don't have a good aerobic base, you may not be ready to race.

- Eating on race morning is very individual. Experiment during a hard training workout or a low-key race to determine what works best. For many athletes, drinks or bars work very well in place of a meal. However, avoid high-sugar foods and drinks since these will adversely affect fat-burning during the race, reducing endurance.

Implementation

Racing is an experience. All other factors being equal, the more you do it, the more successful you will be.

There are so many specific factors relating to each type of race, and other aspects relevant to distance, intensity, altitude, weather, etc. However, there are some key factors which can make a significant difference in your race results.

Whether you're competing in a 5K or a six-day running race, a long bike tour, a short road race, or swimming the English Channel, the first rule of competition is, don't start too fast. This forces your body to burn more sugar, running the risk of depleting your glycogen stores early, which will cause your fat-burning to diminish too.

Starting some races at a comfortable pace, perhaps just faster than your average speed for the race, is the most practical solution. It may take discipline to avoid getting caught up with the pack — most of whom will go out too hard. But don't worry, you'll pass them later in the race. This may not always work in events such as cycling — more of a reason to warm up well.

For some events going out slower for the first part of the race works even better. You'll build your speed throughout and finish very strong. In this instance, athletes often say it's the most fun they've had racing.

Another important component of competition is learning how to relax. The start of any event can have you overanxious and gripped with tension. Just think about standing there waiting for the start. Your heart rate is high, you're tense, and your breathing is fast and shallow. While some of this energy is important for the race, much of it is an overstatement by the mind and a drain of energy.

From the moments before the race starts, focus on your breathing and relaxation. If you're successful at this, your form will be better, you'll have a lower heart rate and your times will improve — all from being more efficient.

Perhaps you require a physical focus on race day; write the word "breathe" or "relax" on your hand or arm where you can easily see it. Or tell yourself that whenever you see a yellow line (on the road), water, or any visual cue, your body will breathe and relax properly (a technique used in hypnosis).

Another successful and very important strategy is to avoid high peaks in your heart rate during the race. This can only be done if you're using a heart-rate monitor unless you're very experienced.

The heart rate normally increases when you are ascending a hill or speeding up, sometimes dramatically. For example, you may be riding along on the road averaging 150 heart rate, when suddenly you begin to climb a steep grade. Your heart rate can also climb as well, sometimes to 170, 180 or to its maximum level.

In a shorter event, this poses less of a problem. But in longer races it can have devastating effects on your energy, using up too much sugar and glycogen. If this is done too early in a long event — even one lasting only an hour or two — you may risk running out of fuel later in the race.

That doesn't mean you should let the pack out of your sight or slow to a crawl at every hill. If you've built enough aerobic speed you'll be able to ascend hills at a good pace without the heart rate rising to maximum levels. In some events, such as running or a triathlon, you'll allow the athletes with you to get ahead, only to catch them soon afterwards having used less energy to get to that same point.

However, in some long events, like an Ironman-distance triathlon, riding at your maximum aerobic heart rate and never higher during the bike portion is essential to maintain sufficient energy and still have enough left for an effective marathon.

For runners, a potential loss of energy during a race comes from over-striding. For some reason, when fatigue builds, many athletes want to reach out with their legs, as if they'll go farther with the same energy. Instead, as you stride longer your body uses more energy as indicated by a higher heart rate. The best recommendation is to allow your stride length to be governed by your body and its energy levels rather than by your image of what you should look like.

Another common problem encountered by competitors during or just prior to a race is experimentation. Some athletes even decide to change their routine right in the middle of a race. That's fine if the purpose of your race is to experiment, whether it's different gears or bike setup, new running shoes or a novel race strategy.

Although all of the above items are very important in the implementation of your race, the most important issue during a race is hydration. Consider the fact that by the end of an endurance event, most athletes are dehydrated to the point where it adversely affects performance. So the simple action of drinking water is vital for a good race. The best rule is to drink as much as you can.

Recovery

Successful racing does not end at the finish line, even for winners. The final step — recovery — enables your body to "heal" from the race, obtain benefits, and prepare you for the resumption of training, or even the next stage. Recovery is also the first step in preparation for your next race.

Recovery involves the physical, chemical and mental aspects of your body. Of the two forms — active and passive recovery — the active type is preferred for the endurance athlete and is discussed here. Passive recovery is reserved for more severe or first-aid situations, or for competitive intensities that are very low, such as golf.

One of the significant benefits of a proper recovery is the ability to speed the reduction of blood lactate to normal levels. This occurs while blood is circulated through the liver, where lactate is broken down. While this normalization of blood lactate occurs relatively quickly under either type of recovery — within about two hours of competition — the sooner it is accomplished the faster you will return to a normal chemical state. The added benefit is that some of your lactate will convert to energy faster.

One problem with moderate or high levels of lactic acid in the muscle is that it changes pH — the acid/base balance. In this state, the body becomes too acid, which can impair energy production and adversely affect muscle contractility. Correction of this acid/base imbalance is accomplished by the breathing mechanism (through increased breathing rate which speeds elimination of carbon dioxide). Natural bicarbonate in the blood also helps counter the increased acidity, assisted by hemoglobin and blood proteins. The kidneys also play a major role in acid/base balance.

The first phase of race recovery is your cool-down. Walking, easy jogging, spinning on your bike, or swimming is a very effective way to aid recovery. Fifteen to 20 minutes is usually enough for most events. Intensity should be very low; do not exceed about 70 percent of your maximum aerobic heart rate. For example, if your maximum aerobic rate is 140, your recovery heart rate should not exceed about 100, but can be below this level. This can be done immediately following the race, or you can wait until you hydrate and consume some nutrients. Be sure to wear your heart-rate monitor to ensure you're not overdoing it while cooling down. It's often more difficult to gauge body intensity following a hard effort.

In some long events, such as an Ironman distance triathlon, even a few minutes of walking — sometimes in a pool — can be very therapeutic and can speed recovery.

In the evening after the race, another short walk, easy spin or swim can also greatly speed recovery.

Walking is especially helpful if you have a long trip home — when you may be sitting for some time. If you're on a plane, walk at the airport and on the plane. If you have an extended drive, stop to take a walking break.

Getting in cool or cold water is also a very good therapy for recovery. It assists in the healing of over-taxed muscles and other soft tissues by increasing circulation and cooling otherwise overheated areas. A local stream, lake or even bath can work wonders, even if only for five minutes.

Post-race food and drink is also important for recovery. Many people can speed glycogen replacement by drinking about 80 grams of liquid carbohydrate within 15 minutes following competition. But be sure to drink plenty of additional water with it.

No matter how much you consumed during the race, you're probably still dehydrated, and will remain so for 24 hours or more. Avoid alcohol, which increases dehydration, until you have consumed lots of water and eaten a meal. Salty foods or drinks with sodium are also important and will help replace the often large amounts of sodium lost in sweat, especially following long events.

The day after your race is an especially important time for recovery. Perhaps an easy swim or walk in the morning, or an easy spin or swim later in the day. No hard or long workouts. If you recover well by the end of the day after a Sunday race, you can resume normal training on Tuesday. In the case of a long event like an Ironman or long bike tour, it will take many more days to recover. Allow your body all the time it needs.

If you're ready to race, successfully following proper preparation, implementation and recovery procedures will ensure you of success.

What if you're not ready to race? Don't. You'll have to sacrifice at least part of the season and get back on track. Modify and correct your training, diet or whatever needs improvement, until you are ready.

Case History

Steve came to me with chronic injuries accompanied by a variety of other overtraining symptoms. Since it was now early May, his main concern was the start of the racing season. But my consideration was for Steve's health. So the season, I explained, had to be modified. We had to correct his injuries and start building a base, which would take three months. If all went well, the plan was to start racing in July. Everything did go well, and Steve had some of his best racing ever from mid-July through early October.

Traveling to Your Race

If you're flying to your race, there are specific factors related to preparation that you may want to consider.

While short airline flights are not too stressful, longer excursions can beat you up, both physically and mentally. Here are some basic tips for air travelers to help overcome the strain — which may have an adverse effect on your race.

- Eat a good meal before going to the airport, and pack some food too. Just pretend you're going on a picnic. You may not get any other acceptable food for some time.

- Arrive at the airport early to avoid the crowds, long lines and stressed people — the stress could wear off on you. Use the extra time to relax, read a newspaper or go for a walk.

- If you're looking for. leg room, get an exit-row seat. But if you don't check in early, they'll all be taken.

- While waiting for your flight, remain in a secluded area — like an empty gate lounge — to avoid annoying or stressed people, and their germs.

- Stay on your feet while waiting for boarding — you may be sitting for some time.

- Drink water throughout your trip. The low humidity in the plane's cabin dehydrates you quickly. Bring water with you. Hot tea (herbal — bring your own bags) works best because it helps humidify your sinuses.

- Avoid coffee, tea, soda and other beverages with caffeine, which speeds dehydration. Alcohol also dehydrates you quickly in a low-pressure cabin.

- When making connecting flights, spend some time walking around to keep loose. This will be easier if your carry-on luggage has wheels.

- Walking around at the airport will be more convenient if you check your bags (but always carry your personal items and a change of clothing just in case your luggage gets lost). Also, try to get outside in the fresh air, assuming the air is fresh around the airport. This is easier if you check your carry-ons into an airport locker.

- On long flights, give yourself a hand and foot massage.

- On long flights, especially to important races where rest is a priority, use your frequent-flyer miles to upgrade to first class (or business, if available). Or purchase a first- or business-class seat. This will make your trip less of a burden because the seats are bigger with more leg room, the food is much better, and there are fewer lines. But the bottom line is you're treated better and you'll arrive less stressed and ready to race.

15

Making Your Own Race Season

In many endurance sports, competition has become a year-round activity. Runners, for example, can find a race within a short drive of home just about any time of year. Fortunately for most athletes, seasons are restricted, mostly due to the weather. But even in this case, the race season is often a long one, with many races crammed into it. And still other situations exist; if you're a pro, you may just pack up your gear and head south or north when the weather changes, and suddenly you're in a different environment and a new race season.

Whatever your situation, at some point you'll need to make your own racing schedule. All it takes is a little planning and discipline.

If you live in cooler areas, where autumn is the end of many race seasons, the weather does half your job of scheduling. In the northeast United States, for example, most race seasons begin with the onset of nice weather — usually April or May. The competitions continue until the cool temperatures begin, usually around the end of October or even November.

This race season, from mid-spring to mid-autumn can be about five to eight months. That's too long for any endurance athlete to maintain health and race well throughout. So breaking up this time frame is the next consideration. The best and simplest way to do this is to take a break from racing in the middle of the season, essentially breaking up your race year into two seasons.

Your first season is from April or May through June or mid-July, and your second season begins mid- to late August through October or

November. Adjust this to your specific race dates. But the most important aspect is your midsummer break.

This midsummer period is a time to build another aerobic base. It's short but sufficient to develop more aerobic function while providing you with sufficient rest and recovery. By taking this break after the first season, you can have a better second season. And in many sports, the more important races are scheduled in late summer or autumn.

The midsummer aerobic base should be no less than about four weeks, with six or eight being reserved if the race schedule is very busy. The more races in the first season, the more time you need to recover. And, the more important the second season is to you, the more added base you'll need.

Case History

Sue is a triathlete who ends her race year with the Hawaii Ironman Triathlon. Here is her typical schedule:

Winter base continues through mid-April
Last two weekends in April: short running race (10K, 5K)
Three weekends in May: duathlons
Three weekends in June: triathlons (last one being a half-Ironman)
July to mid-August: aerobic base
Last two weeks in August: triathlons
Early September: half-marathon running race
Mid-October: Ironman race

Sue may also compete in a couple of running races in mid-November before beginning her long winter base.

If you live in Australia or New Zealand, the Caribbean or Hawaii, or even Alaska, you can make your own schedule to match the local weather, the races and your own life. And if you're fortunate enough to move with the seasons, you can still do the same. Just don't try to race too much in the United States from spring through fall, and then race even more in Australia during that hemisphere's racing season (while the United States has its fall and winter).

In general, if you rely on racing to get your anaerobic stimulation, you can race a little more. In other words, if you perform anaerobic workouts you can't race as often without creating excess stress.

One important consideration regarding your race schedule is extremes in the weather. In Arizona, for example, there may not be as many races or you may not want to race as much in the summer. During this time, even morning temperatures can be in the 90s or 100s. If you're racing locally, you may want to use the summer as your long base period. In this case, break your winter into two seasons. One problem with this is the case where you may want to travel north for one or two big races. These are usually held in the summer, and if that's your base time you may not want to race then.

If you've built at least one good long base (i.e., December through March), had a good racing season, and stayed healthy, you may want to consider some added races in the off season. This is an exception to the rules discussed earlier. During your next long base period you can race occasionally — perhaps once or twice — without ill effects. Let me repeat the criteria:

1. You've already built at least one long base period.

2. You had a good race season

3. You were healthy throughout both base and race season. This means you performed well and did not get injured or run down. If this is the case, racing once or twice during your long winter base (as opposed to the short summer one) should not take away from your health or fitness. And, you should be able to race extremely well.

16

Anatomy of an Injury

Every athlete's worse nightmare is to become injured. Most of us have grown up with a very simplistic view of an injury; you overwork part of your body and it gets hurt. Or, you feel being injured is part of the game. In endurance sports, that's just not so.

For the endurance athlete, an injury should never happen. The only exception is trauma, such as when you've crashed your bike or twisted your ankle. But in endurance activities, injuries are not part of the game like they are in contact sports. Most important, having an injury means you've done something wrong in your training, diet, nutrition or stress management.

Athletic impairment can be described as three basic types: mechanical, chemical and mental injuries. While they overlap most of the time, for illustration I will discuss each separately. Let's dissect an injury to find out where it came from and how it got there.

The Mechanical Injury

You awaken for your morning workout, and as you bend to get into your shoes you feel a little twinge in your right hamstring. Nothing more than that. But several days later, there it is again, now a bit more prominent. And that evening, the twinge has become more than an annoyance and is now beginning to be painful. The next day's workout is hindered, and by the following week, real pain. Now your hip doesn't seem to move right and your knee is throbbing. After another week, all the pain has settled around the knee. You recall no trauma, your shoes seem good, and you've not changed training routines.

This "domino effect" takes place in millions of athletes throughout the world. An injury begins from some seemingly benign event and evolves into real impairment. But there's logic to your body. Events are not random happenings. As Einstein said, "God doesn't play dice." An injury is, with some exceptions, simply an end result of a series of dominoes falling over. One little, innocuous problem affects something else, and the dominoes start to fall. The end result is, sometimes after a half dozen or so dominoes have fallen, a symptom — pain, dysfunction, loss of power, all depending on how the body adapts and compensates to the falling dominoes.

Let's go back to our "typical" injury, and use the one above: knee pain. This is one of the most common athletic injuries. From a professional standpoint, there are two views when confronted with a knee problem.

The traditional view, and in recent decades the more popular approach, attempts to name the condition. If the pain is more lateral and especially a bit above the knee joint, it may be called "iliotibial band syndrome." If it's just below the knee and in the front, especially in a younger athlete it may be called "Osgood-Schlatter." And if the pain is more medial, perhaps it's referred to as a meniscus tear. While these conditions, especially the latter two, are real and serious, and sometimes do occur, even when these conditions are ruled out, their names are sometimes still casually used. This senseless attempt to name these symptoms tells nothing of how the problem occurred, how to fix the problem, and how to prevent it from returning once it is corrected.

This approach also assumes each "bursitis" is exactly the same, or every "tendinitis" is identical. And, modern medicine too often has an off-the-shelf treatment for each name — from rest to stretching, heat to cold, from anti-inflammatory drugs to surgery. The exception is when you are in a "first-aid" state — in this case, none of what I'm discussing applies. Instead, I am referring to the more common chronic injury that most endurance athletes develop.

The most indefensible aspect of this cookbook approach is the fact that many professionals know what they're going to do to you before they even see you. They merely look up the name of your problem in the medical books and find your remedy. It's a classic case of treating the symptom and ignoring the cause — not to mention the athlete attached.

The alternative view is to look at the whole athlete. And, much like Sherlock Holmes, piece together the circumstances that led to the big event, the end-result symptom. These clues provide vital information on how the problem was created, and therefore how to avoid it in the future and how to correct the real cause of the problem. With this approach, each injury is seen as part of the athlete. And each athlete is seen as a unique individual with specific needs which are most appropriate for his or her precise condition. Anything less is an insult to the human body.

So just how does the symptom of knee pain evolve? Of course, our example is just one athlete's paradigm. The same knee pain in a dozen athletes could easily have a dozen different patterns. But let this one serve as an example, taking away the oversimplified view and replace it with a real-life scenario.

Our athlete awakens one morning, puts on his shoes for a workout and feels the first symptom — the twinge in the hamstring muscles. But this is not the beginning of the problem. The first domino fell, perhaps, long before this first manifestation, possibly months earlier.

Perhaps it was the left foot — the opposite side of the eventual symptomatic knee — that underwent microtrauma due to the training shoe not fitting properly. This is a common problem which results in biomechanical stress in the foot and ankle. While this produced no symptoms, it did affect, in a very adverse way, the mechanics of the left ankle. As is often the case when there is this type of mechanical stress on the body, the brain senses the problem and attempts to adapt. In this case, perhaps compensation takes place through the bones and muscles in the pelvis. Specifically, the pelvis tilted to modify its movement so that weight-bearing decreased on the side of stress, and increased on the opposite side — where the symptom will eventually take place. But not yet.

The increased weight-bearing on the right side — usually measurable by standing on two scales — may cause some of the muscles in the thigh to become overworked. This is also partly due to the gait change resulting from the tilt in the pelvis. This causes a right "secondary compensation." Due to the mechanical stress in the pelvis, the quadriceps muscles may, through an unsuccessful attempt at compensation, become weaker or inhibited. And finally, the opposite muscles — the hamstrings — compensate to the quad problem by tightening.

Bending forward to put on your right shoe requires the hamstrings to stretch. But when they are too tight and you ask them to do their job anyway, they could become overstretched with slight microtears. This is the form of that slight twinge.

So what could we propose as therapy in our knee-pained athlete? Anti-inflammatory drugs? Ice the knee? The answer is obvious now that the whole picture is apparent. Find and correct the cause of the problem. In our case here, the first domino to fall was a shoe that was not right for the foot that went into it. (This doesn't mean that all knee problems are the result of shoes.) Whether all the dominoes will line up on their own if you pick up the first one depends on the athlete and how much damage was done. Generally, the body has a great natural ability to heal itself. And in many cases, this is what most often takes place when the cause of the problem is corrected.

This is associated with prevention. How can you avert problems before they begin? Consider that many athletes, when questioned about their injuries, often comment about clues such as their shoes may not fit. It may be a passing thought, a subconscious note. But it's there. And most athletes possess this ability, but unfortunately most also ignore or can't read it. Learning how to read your body only comes with time, but it is worth the effort.

More importantly, when your body gives you a very obvious sign, such as a hamstring twinge, it's time to stop and assess what's going on. If you don't, it may soon be too late. Waiting until you're physically unable to train — the point at which your body forces you to stop — just results in more unnecessary damage and wasted time.

And finally, consider that this whole process, from the time the first domino fell, may take weeks or months, and in some cases, years. And throughout this entire process, your performance is adversely affected.

The Chemical Injury

You spend most of your spare time training, and you're juggling work and family/social life with your sport. Going for a ride is as common as going to bed at night. But now it's getting harder to get through the day due to fatigue. Training no longer energizes you. You're more irritable than ever.

The few pounds you've gained, the first in some time, are probably due to the ravenous appetite you recently acquired. And you're on the forth cold in six months. If you could only sleep as well as you used to. "Luckily I'm not injured," you tell your training partners.

Well, my friend, you are injured. This is not the usual type of mechanical impairment we're most familiar with, such as knee pain. This is a chemical injury.

Chemical injuries typically don't produce the pains like their mechanical counterpart. Although some may provide symptoms of inflammation which can be painful. More often, and by far the most common characteristic of a chemical problem, is it makes you tired. Either the cause of the problem, or the fatigue itself, may in turn produce other chemical symptoms like the ones just described.

As we did above, let's look at the options open to the athlete with these symptoms. Here is the evidence: fatigue, irritability, increased weight gain and hunger, colds and insomnia.

As with any injury, the first step is to rule out more serious conditions, such as anemia, infections or other disorders. This is often easily done with the right blood tests, and the proper history and physical exam by a professional. And when the lab reports and everything else is found to be normal, we've taken the first step in the right direction. Genuine diseases most likely don't exist.

Once diseases are ruled out, more conservative methods can be considered. But wait, we must consider whether our patient is making all this up in her head. Is it an emotional memory she's having related to a past experience? An unpleasant episode with training wheels as a youngster? Let's conclude this is not the case.

Our athlete, who has compiled an inventory of symptoms that are adversely affecting her lifestyle, usually has a common chemical scenario of cause and effect.

Perhaps the problem originated when her schedule became too busy. It wasn't just the training log, but all of life's time commitments, which pushed her over the edge. A key word above, the actual word used by the athlete, gives a vital clue: "juggling." Our athlete was squeezing into her schedule all the items of the day, including the training. For many, this offends the body's ability to properly recover. And as the months went by, a recuperative deficit built up. Perhaps a better word is "stress." The body's adrenal system is designed to adapt and compensate for all this stress, but sometimes the load is just too great.

So, let me piece together the possible events leading to the athlete's chemical injury. Perhaps it was some early success in racing that led our athlete to increase her training. Undoubtedly, total workout times were not only increased, but so was the intensity. With that, the added stress of rushing the meals, and dashing from home to work, workout to home, etc. You know what I mean.

Initially, the increased stress was tolerated well by the adrenal glands. After all, that's their job. But like a long event you're not trained for, the vicious cycle of work, family and social life, training and racing got faster and more difficult to keep pace. Soon, there was less time to do the things that needed to get done, and recovery was hindered. And because she attempted to keep up with her schedule, eventually her adrenal glands became less effective at dealing with all the stress. At this point, recovery may come to a halt.

With the adrenals not able to keep up, the bodily functions it maintains begin to decline. The blood sugar becomes more unstable, which may produce symptoms of fatigue. Also, as the brain is deprived of the sugar it needs, cravings and increased hunger follows. And not only is the brain sensitive to relatively small changes in blood sugar, but the whole nervous system. As such, irritability may follow.

Because of the influence the adrenal glands have on other hormone systems of the body, we may find our athlete's metabolism falling. With this may come a shift in fuel usage, to more sugar and less fat. This can result in more stored fat, and often decreased endurance. Now our athlete has to work harder to keep pace even in training. And race results become even more frustrating. Inevitably, hunger intensifies and fatigue worsens.

Excess adrenal stress is frequently accompanied by decreased immunity. With the body's defense system suppressed, colds and flu, and even allergies become more common, and chronic.

And finally, falling off to sleep may be easy, since fatigue often turns to exhaustion in the early evening. But in many with excess adrenal stress, cortisol — one hormone that's overproduced — oddly wakens the person in the middle of the night full of the wrong energy. Falling back to sleep becomes difficult.

Like any problem you encounter, correction first involves finding the origin. While many therapies may help remedy the symptoms, the real cause may linger unless it is dealt with. After all, a symptom is by definition just evidence. You don't want to treat your evidence, you want to address the cause.

For example, nutritional support for our athlete might include everything from vitamin A for the immune system to zinc for the adrenals. But if the lifestyle schedule, which may have created the original stress, is not modified, problems can continually recur somewhere in the person's chemistry — as either the same set of symptoms or a gathering set of new ones.

This is a typical scenario of a chemically injured athlete. It began innocently enough with a busy schedule, which chemically overtaxed an unsuspecting adrenal system. It continued by producing fatigue, hunger, irritability and colds.

For some, however, this common primary chemical problem may lead to secondary mechanical symptoms, a different cause but much like the symptoms portrayed in the mechanical example above. Unfortunately, these end-result symptoms, secondary to chemical stress, are often seen as the chief problem because they are most apparent. That is why many therapies don't work on a given individual — the real problem is never found and the body cannot heal.

The Mental Injury

For others less fortunate, the chemical injury may also trigger an impairment on a mental or emotional level. When we think of mental problems, visions of psychological tension and emotional instability come to mind. But we should distinguish the mental state from the psychological, and realize that many athletes struggle with mental and emotional distress, but are psychologically stable. The terms mental and emotional refer to a person's behavioral aspect. If the brain gets distorted, from the chemical effects of diet, nutrition or training, a mental injury may result. The problem is not uncommon in the athletic community.

Robert was in his third year of sheer athletic greatness. His training never felt better, and in a race, he was nearly unbeatable. Always full of energy, and without injury, Robert was climbing the ladder to national success.

But in recent months, Robert has become more depressed. And now, his anxiety is more evident, as is his dread of competition. He is not only losing his desire to train, but his personal life is being affected as well.

While Robert is not this athlete's real name, his mental injury is authentic.

There are several ways the brain can be injured in the absence of disease. A functional imbalance in the brain's chemistry — a subtle yet noticeable change in certain substances called neurotransmitters — can modify the way you think, feel and act. Fortunately, with few exceptions, these problems are reversible. And more importantly, preventable.

These brain imbalances may be caused by a mismatched diet, a lack or excess of certain nutrients, or the end result of overtraining. Let's look at what may have happened to Robert in the months before his mental injury. But first, a quick look at how physical your mental state can be.

Normally, when you think a thought or perceive a sensation from the outside world, it's the result of major chemical reactions in the brain. Billions of messages are sent throughout the brain and body on a regular basis because of chemicals called neurotransmitters.

Different neurotransmitters in the brain make you feel certain ways: high, low, sleepy, awake, happy, sad. Sometimes the brain may have too many of one type of chemical or not enough of another. As a result, you may feel too high or too low, agitated or depressed.

Most of the 35 or more neurotransmitters are made from amino acids derived from dietary protein and often influenced by the amount of dietary carbohydrates via the hormone insulin. Two important neurotransmitters are serotonin and norepinephrine.

Serotonin is produced with the help of the amino acid tryptophan, and requires the hormone insulin. This neurotransmitter has a calming, sedating or depressing effect in the brain. A high-carbohydrate meal, such as pasta or oatmeal, or eating sweets, results in more serotonin production. So, the individual who is overactive may benefit from a high-carbohydrate meal, but those who are a bit low to start may get worse, even to the point of depression. Sweets are traditionally thought of as providing energy, but in actuality they are sedating. (Sometimes, sweets may give the feeling of a pick-up but that is very short-lived.) In Robert's case, the overproduction of serotonin — a common problem even in athletes — helped establish his mental injury.

Norepinephrine is produced with the help of the amino acid tyrosine, if little or no insulin is present. A high-protein meal with little or no carbohydrates will provide the brain with increased norepinephrine levels. This neurotransmitter has a stimulating effect on the brain. The person who needs a pick-up or is depressed could often benefit from more of this brain chemical.

An imbalance in serotonin and norepinephrine — with a shift toward the former — may produce depression. Perhaps Robert was eating too many sweets and other carbohydrates, which made him more depressed. Let's look at the therapeutic options available to him.

Certain drugs are sometimes recommended for patients with chemical imbalances because they can manipulate brain chemistry in the hopes of creating a balance of neurotransmitters. The depressed athlete may be given medication to enhance or block certain neurotransmitters. Prozac, elavil and tofranil are examples of anti-depressants which affect the balance of serotonin and norepinephrine, thereby changing the way you feel. (Tranquilizers, such as Valium and Ativan, function other ways through different neurotransmitters.)

Fortunately, most people do not need medication. But if you are overactive or depressed, you may benefit by simply altering your diet to modify your brain chemistry in the most appropriate way. In Robert's case, decreasing the amount of sugar and other carbohydrates in his diet, and increasing protein foods may be of great value.

If the diet can affect the mental state, then clearly certain nutritional supplements can do the same. That's because specific vitamins and minerals — along with the appropriate amino-acid precursors — are required for the brain to make both serotonin and norepinephrine. Some of the more common ones include vitamin B6, folic acid, niacin, iron and vitamin C. But more important are the amino acids tryptophan and tyrosine. All these nutrients — except for tryptophan — are available over-the-counter. (Tryptophan was banned by the FDA a few years ago due to contaminated sources which made some people ill.) The bottom line: Taking too many serotonin-precursor nutrients, including a high-carbohydrate diet, may contribute to a mental injury.

Robert's training may also have contributed to his mental injury. Especially if he was overtrained which results in a stress on his nervous system and emotional instability.

Overtraining frequently is preceded by too much anaerobic work. While we're familiar with the relationship between lactic acid and anaerobic exercise, most have not heard of its effect on the mental state. For a long time, scientists have known that increased lactic acid — more specifically, lactate — in the body may provoke depression, anxiety and phobias.

This occurs due to an overstimulation of the adrenal glands (and occurs with the release of endorphins) and an over-excitation of the nervous system — the same pattern seen in overtraining. It has even been shown that infusion of lactate into relatively normal subjects produces anxiety, depression and panic.

Given this, perhaps Robert produced too much lactic acid from training or racing.

Fortunately, Robert can get himself out of his crisis. While it's not impossible for him to do it alone, more than likely he'll find it easier if he gets help from a friend, family member or professional. Whatever the case, it's important to look at the whole picture.

The big picture includes what happened at the onset. Was Robert training beyond his ability? Was he racing too much, or eating improperly? More often it's a combination of actions. Sitting down and assessing each aspect of his life is a good first step for Robert. Being objective is the hard part — and that's where other people are helpful. Accepting that there really is a problem may also be a difficult hill to climb.

Making the appropriate changes, whatever they may be, can often result in a speedy remedy. Within a couple of weeks, or sooner, Robert can be feeling better, and portray noticeable changes to others around him.

17

Mending Your Own Injury

"The doctor who treats himself has a fool for a patient." I recall that comment from my later years in school. The same holds true for the athlete. It's very difficult to be as objective with your own ills as someone else can be.

But for years, I've also encountered countless athletes who sought care for simple injuries but could not be helped. There are many good doctors and therapists around. But unfortunately, there are many more incompetent ones.

When you're injured, or when you feel something is heading that way, the ideal scenario is to seek the help of a professional. This may be in the form of a doctor, massage therapist, physical therapist, etc. As long as your problem is corrected — I should say the cause of your problem — with no side effects, it doesn't matter what methods are used.

Often I am asked: "What can I do for my _____?" You fill in the blank: iliotibial band syndrome, knee problem, back pain, etc. The list is long.

Physical injuries are an epidemic in the athletic population. One general reason is overtraining. By far the best way to solve this chronic problem of injuries is to prevent them. But that doesn't help the thousands who are right now afflicted with some injury.

Here's the first step; don't treat the name. That's assuming the serious medical problems have been ruled out and there's no need for first aid care. There's no cookbook cure for iliotibial band syndrome or low-back pain. The reality is that everyone's ITB problem is different. So from the start, let's forget about the name — it has hardly any worthy meaning.

Instead, let's find out what the problem is, or is not. In addition, let's discuss what you can do to help your body correct its own problems. After all, that's what your body is supposed to do.

Generally speaking, most injuries are not serious. However, if they are not corrected and continue to prevent you from training, they may end your athletic career.

What I want to say is that most injuries are functional rather than pathological. Functional problems are likened to your car not starting — there's some relatively minor problem which is easily corrected by the right mechanic, if you can just find the right mechanic.

A pathological problem is one in which you need a new engine, or a new car — the problem is often very serious. A broken bone, a tumor, or an injury that can only be corrected by a surgical procedure, is usually a more serious problem. In general, these conditions require more radical care rather than conservative treatment. Fortunately, pathological problems in endurance athletes are not common. Unfortunately, many athletes and professionals use words which describe pathological problems when the injury is simply functional.

Functional problems are often soft-tissue injuries, ranging from simple muscle imbalances to minor ligament or tendon strains or sprains. As opposed to pathological injuries, functional problems are usually correctable with more conservative measures, and quite often by the person who has them.

So what can you do to help correct your own injury? Here are some general suggestions that have been proved successful over time. Don't underestimate the simplicity of these items. Most injuries have simple remedies.

- Find an activity that does not aggravate the problem, and do it. One of the worst problems with the injured athlete is inactivity. This lack of training ultimately can become an aggravating factor. Walking is a great remedy if it doesn't hurt. Running in a pool is also good. Four feet of water will provide some but not too much gravity stress. Stationary equipment sometimes works well (just make sure it's set up or adjusted to fit your body). Try to spend the same amount of time doing these activities (or combi-nations) as you would spend during your normal workout.

If you have pain as part of your injury picture, let it guide you. The best rule to follow regarding pain is that if it improves as your workout progresses, that's generally a good sign. If the pain isn't exacerbated following the activity, that's even better. But if the pain get worse with your activity, stop. Either try anoth-er activity or wait a couple of days and try to work out again, fol-lowing the rules below.

- Make sure you warm up properly with all your activities. Both warming up and cooling down have therapeutic effects on your entire body — from your muscles to your metabolism. In many cases, lengthening your warm-up and cool-down time can also greatly help.

- Avoid stretching. Many injuries are the result of overstretched muscles, with tightness developing as a secondary problem.

- Keep all your workouts strictly aerobic until your injury heals. Be even more conservative with your maximum aerobic heart rate. Avoid all weight-lifting, anaerobic intervals and other hard work-outs, and of course competition.

- Take a good look at your shoes, whether your problem is run-ning-related or not (even the shoes you wear through the day may cause problems). Replace them if there's excessive wear, or if you do not think they fit properly.

- Occasionally, if an athlete could not get to my clinic, I would rec-ommend he or she take three days off as a therapy. Most often, this approach is done before an injury has become extreme, in its early stages. This gives the body a chance to recover and possi-bly correct its own problems. Resumption of training should be cautious for about a week to make sure the problem does not recur.

The most important aspect of an injury is that it should teach you something about your training, racing or equipment. Once you've learned that, you'll become more immune to injuries, and more efficient with training and racing.

18

The Diaphragm: Your Most Important Endurance Muscle

Of all the vital muscles necessary for optimal endurance, perhaps the most important one is the diaphragm. This large flat muscle allows us to breathe; it pulls in oxygenated air and expels unwanted carbon dioxide, a more important item to remove than taking in oxygen.

In well-trained endurance athletes, the breathing mechanism may be the weak link in good performance. In this case, less air enters the lungs, and the blood does not receive the proper amount of oxygen necessary to function up to the levels of the rest of the body.

The diaphragm is also directly associated with other muscles, particularly the psoas major muscle. This most important hip flexor attaches to the diaphragm. Muscles between the ribs, the intercostals, and some of the neck muscles are also important for breathing. During hard activity, 15 percent of the oxygen consumed is used by the breathing muscles. Even at rest, up to 12 percent of oxygen consumption is used for respiration.

An important relationship exists between the diaphragm and the abdominal muscles. Our culture has produced an attitude that makes us overly anxious about our abdominal muscles — specifically, our bellies. Most people think a flat, hard belly is ideal. And many athletes achieve this. But if the abdominal muscles are too tight, it will inhibit the function of the diaphragm, adversely affecting your oxygen intake and carbon dioxide removal. This is a common problem in endurance athletes, and usually results from strengthening by means of sit-ups, crunches and the use of abdominal-exercise machines. Endurance athletes don't want the high-powered steel-like abdominals like we see in body builders. What's more important than looks is the function of the diaphragm.

One of the problems with disturbing the delicate balance between the diaphragm and the abdominal muscles is it often changes the way you breathe. Here is an example of the normal breathing mechanism:

1. During inhalation, the abdominal muscles relax and are gently pushed out, allowing the diaphragm muscle to contract and lower. There is also a simultaneous but slight extension of the spine.

2. Exhalation involves the contracting, or pulling in of the abdominal muscles, with slight flexion of the spine.

3. The chest should move very little during normal breathing, and should expand only during more forced inhalation, and only after the abdominals have relaxed (i.e., are pushed out).

When training and racing, additional expansion of the lungs is necessary. In this case, the chest expands on inhalation, but only after abdominal relaxation and diaphragm contraction.

This sounds easy enough, but many athletes breathe just the opposite way — they pull their abdomens in when inhaling and expand their chests. As a result, less air and oxygen is taken into the lungs, with less carbon dioxide removed. This can be a cumulative stress on the entire system over time — potentially affecting the psoas muscle, hip, low back or other areas of the spine, etc. This is especially important during racing because of the increased need for oxygen and for carbon dioxide removal.

If you're breathing incorrectly, you must first re-learn the normal mechanism. This involves re-training the neurological components of breathing. Stand with one hand on the mid to lower abdomen, and one hand on the lower spine, and slowly practice breathing in and out. Think of the area where your hands are as a vessel, which you are attempting to fill with air.

Another method of training the diaphragm muscle is the straw exercise. This helps improve the power of the muscle, and involves breathing deeply, and slowly, in and out of a straw beginning with 30 seconds. Work up to several sets of one to two minutes each, three times a week for eight to 10 weeks. This may be very difficult at first for someone with a weak diaphragm, but soon you will have no trouble.

Studying yoga or taking singing lessons may also be very effective in building your breathing efficiency, ultimately making your whole body more mechanically efficient.

There are also some simple tests you or a professional can perform to measure diaphragm function.

The Vital Capacity test, which includes various types, is a good method for measuring lung capacity, which reflects general diaphragm function. Vital capacity is related to physiological age. The lower the vital capacity, the older you are physiologically, and vice versa.

A simple test you can do yourself is to measure Breath-Holding Time. This measures the general capacity of the diaphragm, and lung volume. Take a deep breath and see how long you can hold it. Anyone in good health should be able to hold the breath for at least 50 to 60 seconds.

Another test related to the diaphragm is Snider's Test, which measures the strength of the diaphragm using the power or force in the breath. Hold a small lit match six inches away from your mouth. With your mouth wide open, try to blow the match out. You should be able to do so easily.

An important key to endurance training involves making sure your diaphragm muscle functions optimally. Assess it to determine any dysfunction, pay attention to how you breathe during the day and while training and competing, and perform some activity that will improve diaphragm function, such as yoga, singing or other exercises.

19

Your Training Shoes

All shoe companies make good shoes. Your job is to find the right ones for your feet. Modern runners have a choice to make when working out on their feet. It's the decision to wear shoes or train barefoot. Of course almost all choose to wear shoes. But there's a price to pay; wearing running shoes cost you not only in the checkbook, but also in energy and the real possibility of excess biomechanical stress leading to injury.

A little bit of weight added to your feet produces large negative effects in the economy of locomotion. For example, for every 3 ounces of running-shoe weight, a 1 percent increase in oxygen uptake is required.

But the problem goes beyond that. Did you also know that the support systems in almost all shoes can weaken your ankles? And that soft, cushioned shoes can potentially lead to injury? And the thicker the sole the more unstable your foot becomes?

Scientific studies strongly suggest that the protective features put in by shoe companies, including shock absorption and motion control, actually increase the likelihood of injury.

Here are some of the reasons.

The soles of your feet have millions of nerve endings which sense the pounding and stress of walking and running. Your brain and body work together to adapt to this stress by constantly adjusting your gait. This normal protective mechanism keeps you from being injured. When you cover your foot with a shoe, you interfere with this adaptive mechanism. The result is a diminished ability by the foot to adapt, with potential damage to the ligaments, fascia, cartilage or bone in not only the foot, but the leg, thigh, pelvis, low back or many other areas.

Ideally, barefoot is best because there is no interference with the nerves that sense your contact with the ground. Unfortunately, it's not as practical as it once was.

An important fact to remember is this: The impact which results from training occurs whether a shoe is worn or not.

Many shoe support systems, including orthotics, can interfere with the normal functioning of the medial arch. I will only on rare occasions recommend orthotics, and only for a short time while the cause of the problem is corrected.

Sorbothane is a commonly used material in running shoes. While tests on machines demonstrate its great energy-absorbing attributes, a study on humans shows that insoles made of this material actually increase leg stress by 26 percent. Another study showed an increase in foot and leg injuries.

In a study of 5,000 runners, those using more expensive running shoes (those with more shock-absorbing materials) had a higher incidence of injury. So there's no correlation between the pricetag and lesser chance of injury.

Shoes with more cushioning are also likely to produce excessive pronation, especially with the added soft midsole material. Heel height can also increase pronation, especially in shoes with heels that are thicker than about one inch.

But beware: The muscles of your feet and legs, especially the calf muscles, have adapted to the thickness of your shoes. If you suddenly change your shoe style, your muscles may have to re-adjust their length. This may take a couple of weeks, during which you may experience some calf discomfort.

Another problem with higher heels is that it forces you to run too far back on the shoe rather than striking the ground farther forward. This exaggerated heel-toe gait is a walking style and not good or efficient for running.

So now what do you wear?

Basically all the shoe companies make some good running shoes. Try the flat racer/trainer types. In some cases, a racing shoe works well for daily training.

If you're concerned about the steep price of today's shoes, consider other sources. I've been training in a pair of running shoes I get in Wal-Mart or Kmart for under $10.

20

The Short-Shoe Syndrome

L ike overtraining, wearing shoes that don't match the body's needs has become commonplace. A significant number of athletes wear training shoes that are too small. Wearing shoes that are too small can cause pain or dysfunction in the ankle, leg, knee, hip, low back, and at times even in the cervical spine or temporomandibular joint (TMJ).

A study done in my clinic over an 18-month period found 52 percent of new athletic patients were training in shoes too small. Once the problem was diagnosed, these patients usually required a change from ½ to 1½ sizes larger.

Case History

Jim was the classic patient who saw eight different doctors for his problems. Because his symptoms were in both knees, most of the therapeutic attention was directed there. Although his history was unremarkable when first visiting me, his shoes told the story. Jim's right shoe had an area where the large toenail had worn through. Upon measuring his foot, it was found his shoes were a whole size too small. I thought they should be snug, he said. My bike shoes are even smaller. After buying larger shoes, Jim was able to exercise without pain for the first time in more than two years.

Why Foot Sizes Change

You may think that the size of your feet is set by age 20, but this isn't true. Normal size changes, as a result of weight gain or loss, gait problems, muscular imbalance and pregnancy, occur regardless of age. The increase is due to the relaxation or elongation of the ligaments and tendons, followed by an expansion of the bones in the foot. Generally, the more weight-bearing type training, such as running, the greater the likelihood that your feet will become larger after the age of 20. Even if you spend all day at your job standing on your feet, your required shoe size can change.

Some athletes, having bought larger shoes after the initial diagnosis, experienced continued enlargement of their feet, eventually ending with a total difference of up to 2½ sizes!

First Metatarsal Jam

Training in a shoe that's too small — too short in length — results in a slow jamming of the toes, characteristically causing a subluxation of the first metatarsal joint. This creates a mechanical instability in the foot, which if left uncorrected, can lead to other foot and ankle problems such as hammer toes and bunions. In time, the toes become spring-like; when a small shoe is slipped on, the toes spring in, and the tightness of the shoe is not obvious. The first metatarsal joint, however, is not as flexible as the joints of other toes, and therefore takes most of the abuse.

Diagnosing the Problem

Due to the slow onset of this common problem, the first metatarsal jam is often asymptomatic. If you have it, you usually don't complain of pain in that first toe joint.

But visual examination of your feet may reveal trauma, or micro-trauma (long-lasting mild stress) to the front of the foot. This often includes discoloration of the nail bed (black toenail), blistering or callousing of the toes, or swelling of the first metatarsal joint (the ball of the foot). In more extreme cases, inspection of your shoe may reveal wear and tear, inside and out, as a result of the nail or front of the toe trying to push out of the shoe.

Take out and study the insert in your shoe. Look at the wear pattern (the indentation made from the toes) on this insert, and see if the areas compressed by the toes are not completely on the insert. If the foot over-laps the top of the insert, it's obvious that the shoe size is wrong.

The importance of properly fitting shoes cannot be overemphasized. Below are tips on finding the perfectly fitting shoe:

- Measure your foot. After a certain age, people often don't have their feet measured when buying new shoes, since they don't realize their size could have changed. As a result, the same shoe size is worn for years, or even decades. Have both feet measured by a competent shoe-store salesperson. Take this measurement while standing on a hard floor. It may be necessary to have your feet measured two or even three times during the day, due to normal size fluctuations. (Of course, any meaningful daily size fluctuations must be differentiated from serious health problems, such as swelling and certain pathological changes.) Compare the actual size of the foot with the measured size of the shoe currently being worn. However, measuring your foot is not as accurate as you think. Be aware that the size on the measuring devices (a somewhat random unit of measurement), and the size stamped on the shoe may not always match. Indeed, most of the time it's very different. Some shoes run a half or even whole size smaller or larger than other shoes, or compared to the measuring device used in shoe stores. So the bottom line is to go by fit, especially comfort.

- Spend adequate time trying on shoes in the store. Find a hard surface rather than the thick soft carpet found in many shoe stores, where almost any shoe will feel good. If there is no sturdy floor to walk on, ask if you can walk outside. If the shoe salesperson will not allow this, shop elsewhere. Try on the size you normally wear. Even if that feels fine, try on a half-size larger. If that one feels the same (or even better), try on another half-size larger. Continue trying on larger half-sizes until you find the shoes that are obviously too large. Then go back to the previous half-size and usually that's the best one. You may need to try different widths to get a perfect fit, which is what you should strive for. Don't let anyone say that you will have to break them in before they feel good. Even though you may develop the reputation of being a nuisance at your shoe store, your body will benefit. It would also be worth educating the salespeople if they are unaware of these types of problems.

- For those people who have a significant difference of more than a half-size between their two feet, it may be best to wear two different-sized shoes. If this is the case with you, write the shoe company whose shoes you like, and explain your situation. The company may be willing to help. If the difference between the two feet is less than a half-size, fit the larger foot.

- When it comes to training shoes, more women fit and function better in men's shoes than in women's shoes. Rule No. 1 though, is that the shoe must fit properly, and feel completely comfortable. Some women don't fit into men's shoes, and some stores don't carry men's shoes in sizes that are small enough for some women.

- You may not find the right shoe in the first store you go to. Most outlets carry only a few of the many shoes on the marketplace. Often, shoes from mail-order outlets cost less. But be prepared for the hassle of shipping back those that don't quite fit right. Most people will settle for a mail-order shoe that does not quite fit properly, or is not quite as comfortable, in order to avoid returning the shoes.

- Remember, the manufacturer makes new shoes based on trends of style, color and fancy gimmicks used to market the shoe. That is why many shoe models come and go so frequently. So if you finally find the shoe that works great for you, buy several pairs. Just be sure to try them all on, since the same shoe style may vary in size.

21

Women and Endurance

For centuries women have been deceived, cheated and denied their right to use their natural power of endurance. Assorted reasons have not only been given, but were the social norms as to why the female of the human species should not, and could not, be interested in or preoccupied by sports, especially the endurance variety.

Yes, we have most women's sports in most schools. But still there are the holdouts — in cycling, for instance, the Tour de France is without women. Most professional sports are for men only. Until the 1960s, females were prohibited from running races longer than 800 meters. They were also barred from official participation in the marathon until the 1970s, with the first women's Olympic Marathon in 1984. In that race, Joan Benoit's 2:24 would have won 11 of the previous 20 men's Olympic marathons.

Today, the female endurance athlete has arrived, but her acceptance has not really been as complete a success as has the men she races against. At least not yet.

Fortunately, women have gained more equality in endurance events than in many other sports. But in this endurance world, women still have one last step to attain — that of outperforming their male counterparts.

What is generally missed is the fact that women in the endurance field can be equal to or excel over men. It has led scientists to ask if the difference between male and female performance is all biological, or if there is a major social impediment that prevents women from achieving their full endurance potential.

The differences in men and women are obvious; the structural, chemical and mental aspects empower each to function as efficiently as nature intended. But in the natural evolution of the human species, one aspect that was essential to survival was endurance. And men and women developed it equally.

When the topic of the female athlete is brought up, the discussion usually reverts to the power comparisons between male and female, menstrual problems, osteoporosis, eating disorders and other "special" concerns for female athletes. Even the danger of women training alone becomes an issue unique to women. While all these concerns are important, they should not be the primary focus. Nor should their difference be distorted.

Body composition of females is nearly identical to males for the first dozen or so years of life. For example, fat-free body mass averages are the same until about the age of 13. At this time, different hormonal changes between the sexes produce the contrasts we are all familiar with. In the case of the female at puberty, the pituitary hormones trigger the ovaries to develop and produce estrogen. This hormone, among other actions, increases stored fat, primarily necessary for pregnancy and lactation.

In the male at puberty, the same pituitary hormone results in testosterone production. This hormone provides for a larger body frame and muscle mass. But women produce some testosterone as well, and men manufacture some estrogen.

It is the consequences of these hormonal events that allow comparisons between male and female athletes. In addition, other differences are measurable, especially those related to the responses to training. For example, because of the larger quantity of muscle, men tend to be stronger in power. Unfortunately, this leads some to infer that women are the "weaker" sex. (Ashley Montague's *Natural Superiority of Women* looks at this issue in a broader, more natural view.) However, when other factors are considered, such as comparing absolute strength to free fat mass, the differences are much less significant or there are none at all. Women can improve strength dramatically, but without the major increase in muscle mass seen in men. This decreased muscle mass in women is compensated for by improved neurological function.

Endurance sports are not true power events, where muscle bulk is key. If that were the case, just lifting weights would provide the advantage, and almost all men would cross the finish line before even the first woman. But the primary "power" in endurance events comes from aerobic function.

Endurance capacity is often measured using VO_2 max. Females reach their peak VO_2 max in early teens whereas males reach theirs around age 20, and maintain higher levels than women. But the average woman athlete has a VO_2 max that's only 8 to 12 percent lower than the average man. Women are also capable of experiencing the same relative increase in VO_2 max as men.

But endurance events are not won by the athlete with the highest VO_2 max. Nor are these races all-out sprints or power events. So the submaximal oxygen consumption may be of greater importance — not only in the race itself but also in the training required. And when submaximal VO_2 is compared, little if any difference is found between men and women.

Studies done on middle- and long-distance runners show that women's peak lactate values are significantly lower — 45 percent less — than men's. And, when expressed in relative terms, anaerobic threshold values are similar in men and women.

Women possess a greater capacity than men for fat-burning. Improving their metabolism through training and diet to burn more fat may give them the edge, since fat-burning is a key in endurance events. Unfortunately, too many women still adhere to a low-fat diet, which may contribute to ill health, with amenorrhea a common end result. In addition to burning more fat, trained women seem to have lower stress (indicated by lower epinephrine levels) and less muscle-glycogen depletion during endurance training.

How does all this translate into real-life issues of racing? Can a finely tuned woman beat an equally finely tuned man in an Ironman-distance race? If so, will they then change the name to Ironwoman? We may have to wait for the answers, but probably not too long.

Changing tradition and social customs takes time. Only recently (since the '70s) have some young girls developed with as much physical activity as their boy counterparts. And this is still not the norm. Girls are just now beginning to be trained as hard as boys. Once that happens, their performances will improve dramatically and should continue to do so.

If recent history is an indication, we may be seeing more women out-performing more men. In the 400-meter freestyle, the winning time for the women in the 1924 Olympic Games was 16 percent slower than the men. In 1948, this difference shrunk to 11.6 percent, and in 1984 diminished to only 6.9 percent. And the men's world-record time for the 800-meter freestyle set in 1972, was bettered by a women just seven years later.

Other sports follow this pattern of closing the gap in performance. In recent years the second place finisher at the Leadville Trail 100-mile running race was Ann Trason. Her time was 18 hours, 40 minutes — only 6 minutes behind the leader! Paula Newby-Fraser's sub 9-hour Ironman performances are only bested by a very small number of men. And the record for swimming the English Channel is held by a women at 7 hours, 40 minutes. The best men's time is 32 minutes slower at 8 hours, 12 minutes.

Are there really any differences in training and dietary needs for women compared to men, as indicated by advertisers and tradition? In my experience, no. My approach is based on individualization, and I don't use different training methods because the athlete is female. Nutritionally, a women does not need more iron or calcium just because she's a women. Rather, athletes must assess the specific need for iron, calcium and all other nutrients, regardless of sex.

It is my feeling that in the coming years women endurance athletes will improve at a faster rate than will men. More women will break into the top 10 or 20 at races of all levels. And women will start competing for the top spots in the big races.

22

Training at Altitude

For many years, training at altitude has maintained a certain mystique. Cities like Boulder, Colorado, have blossomed as an endurance mecca in part due to the training benefits many believe would come with working out there.

Unfortunately, spending time in Boulder is not the magic ingredient for the improved endurance many seek. Actually, more athletes who go to higher altitudes to train end up overtraining. Part of the problem is due to social factors. But even the moderate elevation of cities like Boulder increases the training heart rate for weeks. If training is based on pace rather than heart rate, most athletes end up training too hard. With the "thinner" air, overtraining often follows.

Going to altitude for whatever reason is a big stress on your body. As soon as you arrive there, oxygen uptake diminishes — the higher you go, the less oxygen your body takes in. Your training performance (submaximal work) is reduced dramatically. Ascending to higher altitudes can be such a stress that a condition called acute mountain sickness can follow, resulting in headache, nausea, insomnia and malaise. And, reduced food intake sometimes does not match your energy expenditure needs, which can be an added nutritional stress. In addition, there is much less moisture in the air, and dehydration is much more common. Your body will compensate to the stress of altitude, at least the oxygen-debt aspect, partly by increasing your heart rate and breathing rate. This enables you to increase oxygen carrying to compensate for reduced oxygen uptake. Over time, the kidney makes more of the hormone erythropoeitin (Epo) which stimulates the bone marrow to make more red blood cells. Eventually, after several weeks, all this compensation enables you to train without the stress encountered when you first arrived at altitude. However, high intensity training, including competition, remains poor relative to sea level conditions.

Being at altitude does come with benefits. But the advantage is in living there, not training there. As a result of taking in less oxygen, the body adapts by producing more red blood cells. This is the result of the hormone erythropoietin. The higher the elevation, the more this process proceeds. In addition, the hemoglobin content in the blood increases as well, all providing an increased oxygen-carrying capacity of the blood. While these benefits are good for your health, it only significantly improves your fitness when, and if, you return to lower altitudes to compete.

Returning to sea level, for example, three weeks before a major race offers the best of both altitudes. First, at the lower altitude your oxygen uptake is greater. And second, you maintain the improved oxygen-carrying capacity developed during your time at altitude, which helps prepare you for competition. This has been Mark Allen's strategy through the years he won his six Hawaii Ironman races.

Another benefit of training at altitude is not a physiological one. The enjoyment of being in most moderate-level mountainous regions is socially and psychologically rewarding. Whether in the Rocky Mountains, in the ranges of the southwest or the northwest corridor, most areas offer a healthy, low-stress place to train and live compared to hurried, tension-ridden areas such as New York or Los Angeles. And, the summer weather in these mountain areas offer additional benefits of being less humid and cooler, a radical change from places like Georgia, Florida and Texas.

Let's look at more of the changes that occur when training at altitude. The air you breath at higher altitudes is the same as the air at sea level; it contains about 21 percent oxygen. The barometric pressure, however, is lower as you ascend in altitude, and the difference creates a decreased ability to get oxygen out of the air.

In addition to oxygen changes, altitude training also imposes other factors that must be considered. Temperature, humidity and solar radiation are the most important.

As you ascend, air temperature drops at a rate of about 1 degree C for every 150 meters. This can be significant when cycling to higher elevations, especially when considering the wind chill. Humidity is also much lower at higher altitudes, since cold air holds much less water. Water loss is increased, from respiratory evaporation due to increased respiration, as well as from water loss through sweating. This poses a potential problem of dehydration, an already frequent dilemma in athletes. Being at altitude increases your need for water significantly and a major effort should be taken to drink more water.

You should also be aware of the solar danger at higher altitude. Because there is less air for the light to travel through, more of it reaches you. In addition, the decreased water in the air, which normally absorbs light, also increases the amount of light that hits your body. And if there is snow, reflective light can amplify this problem as well.

The muscles are also affected by altitude and have difficulty adjusting as well. In general, this is a problem beginning with altitudes above about 1,600 meters (5,248 feet). In this situation, muscle performance is greatly diminished due to the rapid decline of VO_2 max. In addition, muscle enzymes, which regulate energy production, decline, and total surface area of the muscle also is diminished.

One important fact about altitude training is that we don't know everything about it. This leaves empirical information — the observation of what seems to work best — along with the scientific information that is useful.

Here are some of my recommendations for those who want to travel to altitude to train for endurance.

- The ideal altitude for endurance training is between 1,500 meters and 2,000 meters, with the benefits being realized when you return to sea level.

- If you plan to stay at altitude for long periods (such as the summer months), your training should be diminished for the first two weeks of arriving at altitude. For the first two or three days, training should be restricted to easy walking.

- Anaerobic workouts should be minimized at altitude.

- If competing at altitude, train aerobically for at least two weeks at that altitude in order to adapt.

- If you are not able to stay at altitude for two weeks before competition, arrive at your race the night before. Many of the negative physiological changes become significant after the first 24 hours at altitude.

- The optimal state is to live at higher altitudes, and train at lower ones. For example, living and sleeping at 6,000 feet when not training, then driving down the mountain to train.

- A better option is to use a hypobaric chamber, which enables you to get the altitude living benefits without traveling (see Chapter 23).

Perhaps the best recommendation I could make is that if you have the option to train any place you like, choose a location which is most pleasant to live. A more relaxed environment with good weather will do more for you than anything else.

23

Hypobaric Chambers

A t one time, it was thought that obtaining the physiological benefits of high-altitude exposure meant moving to Kathmandu, or at
least Boulder, Colorado. Today, we know that spending small
amounts of time in a hypobaric chamber can bring about the same effects,
while allowing the athlete to train more efficiently in a low-altitude environment.

The most up-to-date research indicates an ideal situation for athletes
is to live at altitude and train at sea level. The altitude benefits can be
achieved with the use of a hypobaric chamber. While long stays at altitude can be helpful, the drawback of added training stress, not to mention
travel expense can be counter productive.

The regular use of a hypobaric chamber may be much more effective
than training at altitude for other reasons as well. Athletes traveling to
altitude often overtrain because they rarely allow their bodies the necessary time to adapt; they either train at the same level as before, or actually increase their training duration and/or intensity.

An altitude simulation chamber allows athletes to get the benefits of
altitude living much more practically and with less disruption to training
programs. The altitude chamber was invented by R. Igor Gamow, the
famed University of Colorado professor who also invented the portable,
mild hyperbaric chamber that bears his name (the Gamow Bag, which is
discussed in the next chapter). The hypobaric chambers are very safe to
use. They are made of acrylic (transparent) or fiberglass, with diameters
of up to 36 inches. They contain a mattress making them very comfort-

able for sleeping all night, or just for a short period of rest or reading. They are about 7 feet long, and weigh about 200-300 pounds. Air is pulled out with the use of a relatively quiet pump, and the pressure, or altitude simulation, is easily and completely controlled by the person inside.

Quick Benefits

The most dramatic benefit of being at altitude is the increase in your body's natural production of erythropoietin (Epo) which begins almost immediately with hypobaric exposure. The production of Epo stimulates the production of red blood cells, which increase the body's oxygen-carrying capacity, or ability to get oxygen to working muscles, by as much as 150 percent. In addition, more blood vessels are developed, less lactate is produced during training and competition, and a significant overall improvement in sports performance can be attained. It's more healthy and natural to increase your Epo this way than to inject synthetic Epo (which is illegal and dangerous) or use other blood-doping methods (also illegal and dangerous).The result is improved oxygen carrying capacity and dramatic performance enhancements — all obtained legally and healthily.

The time necessary to obtain these benefits depends on the individual and the elevation used in the chamber. One study showed significant benefits could begin in as little as 30 minutes — just enough time to catch up on your reading, take a restful breather from life's stresses or just snooze.

The effects of shorter periods of exposure are well substantiated by other research as well. One study showed a three-fold increase in Epo production after only 84 minutes with a hypobaric environment equal to about 13,000 feet elevations. Another showed that nine days of hypobaric exposure, three to five hours per day, resulted in a 3.9 percent performance improvement.

The dramatic effectiveness of hypobaric therapy in athletes might be best exemplified by a group that used a chamber in preparation for an ascent on Mount Everest. The climbers used hypobaric chambers for four days, averaging 9.5 hours per night before their climb. On Mount Everest, the speed of ascent was very high (5,600 meters of altitude gain in six days), whereas in conventional expeditions, 12 to 32 days are generally necessary to safely reach the same altitude.

Increased Athletic Performance

A significant overall improvement in sports performance can be attained through the use of a hypobaric chamber. In addition to increasing production of Epo, and subsequently the body's ability to get oxygen to working muscles, other health and fitness benefits of using a hypobaric chamber include increases in total blood volume, hematocrit, capillaries, mitochondria volume and VO_2 max. In addition, the increased blood volume increases circulation and functional blood vessels.

These benefits translate directly into performance increases. One study demonstrated a nearly 4 percent improvement in running speed after only nine days of using the chamber. For a person who runs a 35-minute 10K race, that would be an improvement of 1 minute and 24 seconds, improving the time to 33:36. For a 3-hour marathoner, this would equate to more than a 7-minute improvement. For a 10-hour Ironman event, it would equate to almost a 9.5-hour time!

Monitoring your training quality and using a heart-rate monitor are important considerations when using an altitude simulator to improve performance. Overtraining and inflammation often go together, which can reduce your Epo production.

Lasting Benefits

It's clear that intermittent hypobaric exposure results in lasting benefits. Precisely how long higher levels of Epo, red blood cells, hematocrit and other measurable factors can be maintained is not known due to individual variation, as well as time and consistency of exposure. One study showed consistent exposure maintained elevated Epo levels for up to 20 days.

The ideal option for an athlete is to monitor progression through blood tests. This may be done using a simple finger prick for some evaluations. More extensive testing is suggested before, during and after hypobaric therapy, and may include the following:

- A complete blood count (CBC) to monitor red-cell count, hemoglobin and hematocrit gives a more complete picture of physiological benefits.

- Testing levels of iron, ferritin, folic acid, and other nutrients provides information to ensure adequate nutrition to obtain optimal benefits from hypobaric exposure.

- The erythrocyte sedimentation rate (ESR) may help rule out inflammation (which inhibits Epo).

Diet and Nutrition

Both diet and nutrition can have a significant effect on the effectiveness of hypobaric therapy in an athlete's program. For this reason, a dietary analysis should be performed on the athlete to ensure proper nutrient intake. Athletes who lack specific nutrients may not improve as dramatically when using the hypobaric chamber, and if this is the case, nutritional supplementation should begin.

In addition, inflammation can inhibit Epo production. For this reason, when using an altitude chamber it's important to consider the powerful dietary nutritional aspects that regulate inflammation, including balancing dietary fats, making sure you get certain vitamins and minerals and adequate protein. It is also important to assess your iron, B12, and folic acid status, and your antioxidant intake as well when using any device that increases Epo.

Some nutrients have obvious potential impact on the athlete's physiology, and this impact becomes even more acute with hypobaric exposure. A variety of specific nutritional factors may further help athletes who use hypobaric chambers to improve health and performance. Below is a list of some:

- Iron deficiency could decrease oxygen-carrying capability.

- Inadequate protein intake could negatively influence Epo production.

- Zinc may be required at levels higher than normal.

- There may be an increased need for antioxidant nutrients for those undergoing hypobaric therapy.

- Folic acid could have a significant effect on the production of red blood cells.

- Folic acid (and vitamin B12) may improve the production of Epo.

- Omega-3 fatty acids may impact the quality of red blood cells produced.

Reviewing the Options

The concept of "live high, train low" can be mimicked with regular use of the hypobaric chamber. In this instance, use the chamber regularly and for as long as is practical during each session. The athlete must balance the practicality, availability and improvement potentials. Here are some options to consider:

- **Ease yourself up.** When using the hypobaric chamber, begin with an 8,000-foot equivalent (likened to airline travel) and increase proportionately to 15,000 feet over several days. This altitude simulation can then be maintained, and may be the ideal level.

- **Maximize effects for competition.** Some athletes may choose to sleep in the chamber for three weeks each night just before key competitions. This may ensure optimal performance benefits in a relatively short period.

- **Build long-term benefits.** An easier choice is to use the chamber for shorter periods, but regularly over a longer period of time. This can provide very similar benefits, but with the added benefit of training for weeks and months with higher red blood counts and oxygen utilization. This can provide the athlete with potentially more benefits from his or her training.

- **Short exposures can be effective.** The time spent in the chamber may be proportionate to the benefits obtained. While sleeping in the chamber every night may be optimal, significant benefits can be achieved with much less exposure — beginning with 60-90 minutes five days a week, for example.

- **Share your hypoxia with friends.** Since shorter periods of expo-sure can be effective, a number of athletes can benefit by sharing one chamber. In this way a group of athletes can cost-effectively schedule individual chamber times throughout the day and evening, for varying amounts of time. In addition, one athlete may also sleep in the chamber during the night (or, some athletes can take turns using the chamber all night). In this scenario, 10 or more athletes could easily obtain benefits from one chamber.

- **Maintain effects with less exposure.** Maintaining the benefits obtained with previous hypobaric exposure can be accomplished with less exposure. It is important for athletes to monitor their performance improvements through use of the MAF Test.

- **Monitor the results.** Blood tests allow more objective monitor-ing of physiological changes. Due to biochemical individuality, responses to the use of hypobaric chambers may vary. It would be optimal for individual athletes to monitor specific indices such as hematocrit to assess improvement. Only then can each athlete determine optimal time requirements in the chamber, and how long optimal benefits can be maintained during periods when the hypobaric chamber is not used.

24

Mild Hyperbaric Chambers

You may have heard or read reports about how hyperbaric chambers have been helpful for patients with severe burns, for bone fractures and even AIDS. Many of these findings seem valid, and the use of hyperbaric chambers is rapidly becoming a mainstream therapy for many other problems. I have used mild hyperbaric chambers since the mid-1980s to help improve overall body function. While hypobaric chambers mimic high altitude, hyperbaric chambers mimic low altitude. As such, they increase oxygen uptake significantly. One does not need to add oxygen to the chamber to accomplish this.

A hyperbaric chamber compresses the inside air, creating a high pressure. In many cases, the larger chambers also contain added oxygen. Mild hyperbaric chambers, developed by Dr. Igor Gamow of Boulder, Colorado, are much smaller, and oxygen isn't usually added to the compressed air. A person in a high-pressure environment can get more oxygen out of the air.

My clinical research has indicated the high-pressure environment of a mild hyperbaric chamber has a significant therapeutic effect on health and fitness through an increase in oxygen uptake and vital capacity, and an increased ability of the body to carry oxygen to all the cells.

Traditionally, hyperbaric chambers were used for first aid. The most common applications include treatment of mountain climbers for altitude-related illnesses, and divers and pilots for decompression sickness resulting from too rapid or extreme a change in pressure exerted on the body. Patients with heart problems and chronic infections, as well as burn victims, have also been treated successfully in hyperbaric chambers.

The mild hyperbaric chamber is a 17-cubic-foot non-permeable nylon cylinder-shaped "bag" with an airtight zipper. This is a portable version of the more elaborate chambers used. It's inflated with an oil-free medical compressor, and the environment is regulated through pressure-controlled vents. A continuous flow of incoming and outgoing air prevents carbon-dioxide buildup.

The higher pressure in the chamber mimics the pressure of low altitude and, to a lesser degree, high-pressure weather systems. So, if you were using a hyperbaric chamber in Boulder, Colorado (altitude 5,000 feet), the pressure inside the chamber would mimic near sea-level conditions. If you were using it at sea level, it would mimic the conditions for 4,000-5,000 feet below sea level.

The most significant fact to be considered is that an increased air pressure equivalent to descending from 1,763 meters to sea level, will increase oxygen uptake by 11.1 percent. A descent of 3,000 meters, or the addition of slightly more pressure, increases the total oxygen uptake by more than 17 percent! This increase is likened to that obtained through daily exercise after many months or even years of training, but is attained while in the mild hyperbaric chamber. The effects can last several days or longer depending on the individual.

Case History

Barbara, 48 years old, had improved since her initial visit to the office five months ago, but still complained of some fatigue and an inability to lose weight. Two months previous, she decided on her own to stop taking the thyroid medication she had been on for the past six years. After three sessions in the mild hyperbaric chamber, her vital capacity improved (from an average of 2700cc to 3400cc), as did her temperature, which was always in the low 96°F range. After the first time in the chamber, her temperature increased to 99.2°F. One week later, Barbara's temperature was 98.6°F, and after two weeks it remained at 98.2°F. She subsequently lost 6 pounds and several sizes, indicating fat loss.

It's common to see athletic performance improve through the therapeutic use of a mild hyperbaric chamber. Other studies have demonstrated that performance levels are increased at lower altitudes and higher pressures. One benefit of living and training at higher altitudes is when you descend to a lower altitude for athletic competition, the relative increased oxygen consumption can improve your performance. Some of these improvements are due to the effect on lactic acid. Lactic-acid production occurs when the oxygen availability is decreased. Given the same exercise stress, with increased oxygen, less lactic acid is produced. This makes the hyperbaric chamber an excellent means of speeding recovery from exercise and competition.

There is a relationship between lactic-acid levels and depression, anxiety and phobias. A significant number of people using the hyperbaric chamber have reported psychological benefits. Some of this subjective information may be placebo effects, but the relationship between high-pressure environments and mental states is clear. High-pressure weather systems are typically accompanied by a feeling of well being. That's why you feel happier and more energetic on sunny, blue-sky days, as opposed to the cloudy low-pressure days when many people are sluggish both mentally and physically.

Case History

Tom is 29, and is very active cycling, running and swimming. He came to the office the morning after a bicycle accident, having been screened the previous evening in a hospital emergency room. Shoulder ranges of motion were very restricted due to pain. He was put in the hyperbaric chamber for 45 minutes. His vital (lung) capacity significantly increased after being in the chamber — from 5,100 to 5,900cc. His temperature was a low 96.8°F before getting in the chamber, and was elevated to a near normal 98.0°F after. Also, several muscles which tested weak due to the accident, tested strong and without pain following his time in the chamber. This improved muscle function also resulted in a dramatic change in posture and range of motion. Tom successfully competed in a local swimming race the following morning. Measurements of vital capacity one week and two weeks later showed a steady level of 5,800 each week.

This emerging field is under-researched because it's underfunded. More laboratory research is needed to find out what other changes take place and what protocols are most useful. In 1990, the U.S. Olympic Committee completed a pilot study using the hyperbaric chamber on elite runners. The research staff included Peter Van Handle, Ph.D., and concluded that "exposure to a hyperbaric environment may improve maximal work capacity."

One of the more interesting aspects of the use of mild hyperbaria is the improvement in the way the body burns fat. It is, after all, the increased utilization of oxygen (one major result of exercise) which results in fat loss. This assumption is an extrapolation from the information available and from the current research.

At this point, no negative effects have been observed as a result of the hyperbaric chamber. Those who use hyperbaric chambers regularly and increase their oxygen uptake, should be aware that improved nutrition must accompany these changes. As the body can take more oxygen out of the air, it's possible that the need for antioxidants may also increase.

Mild hyperbaric chambers are now readily available. MAF group (877-264-2200) is marketing the original "bag" chamber, which can be packed up in a small suitcase for travel.

Hyperbaria and Hyperoxia

Increasing the pressure of ambient air, hyperbaria, as a means of increasing oxygen uptake is not the same as increasing the total oxygen content of air, which is called hyperoxia. However, it has been argued that no difference exists between increased oxygen utilization from hyperbaria and as a result of breathing pure oxygen without hyperbaria. But many experts, myself included, agree that hyperbaria (increased pressure) and hyperoxia (increased oxygen) are not the same. One important difference is in the oxygen and carbon-dioxide levels of the blood flow to the brain. Hyperoxia actually lowers brain blood flow, as well as oxygen use. In general, breathing high concentrations of oxygen can even lower general artery oxygen levels and create an oxygen toxicity, not to mention the dangers of free-radical damage. Any beneficial effects of hyperoxia are also very limited. But the positive effects of mild hyperbaria can last several days to a week or more with one 45-minute period in a chamber.

25

If Einstein Were Your Coach

Whether you're just beginning your endurance career or training for a double Ironman, Albert Einstein would say the key to an effective program is taking charge of the time element. Einstein said, "Time is relative." He postulated that a spacecraft leaving earth and traveling near the speed of light for 20 years would return to earth with a different record of time elapsed than that on earth.

Comparing two identical clocks, one on the spacecraft and one on earth, the spacecraft clock may show 10 years had elapsed, but the clock on earth would show 20 years had passed. Moreover, the passengers on the spacecraft would have aged only 10 years while those on earth had aged 20 years in that same time. This view of two clocks providing us with different times of the same event can be useful in training for endurance.

We all know the human body can sense and react to time differently, given the same situation. A successful race seems to pass more quickly than one in which you are struggling. "Time is not a constant thing by any means," says Olympic marathoner Lorraine Moller of New Zealand. "When you're in a good race, everything comes together. Time flies when you're having fun."

Time can be experienced as a non-flowing, isolated part of any performance; the event does not take place as most see it, but differently. This view of time is most evident when we're falling in love, meditating or in a trance. As Larry Dossey, M.D., states in his book *Space, Time, and Medicine*: "These experiences suggest that an alternative to the ordinary means of experiencing time lies within all of us." In our fast-paced society, we always seem to run out of time. This, among other things, creates stress.

If you're rushing through your workouts, not "taking the time" to enjoy them, this stress may eventually have a negative influence on your overall health and fitness.

Tim is a common example of another kind of time problem. The remedy is something Albert Einstein could provide.

Case History

Tim had been running regularly for five years, and at age 37 was training for his fourth marathon. He was hoping to break the elusive three-hour barrier, which he had been close to in his three previous marathons. His training schedule included the traditional "long" Sunday run of two hours, and would soon increase so that his "longest" run would be two-and-a-half hours. However, relative to even his "longest" run, how will Tim relate to the time it will take him to run the three-hour marathon? In other words, for Tim, two hours was long, two-and-a-half hours longest. Was three hours reasonable? Tim needed to modify his approach or he'd fail to attain his goal, as so many do in events that have significant time factors. He had to relate both psychologically and physiologically to three hours as short.

Einstein was able to understand and relate to complex issues, but how could he help Tim, or anyone else in such relatively simple quests? Using our earlier notion that an event can be viewed through two clocks will help anyone to control time more effectively.

"A lot of coping with time," Lorraine Moller says, "is just learning to relax." You might try relaxing in front of a clock with a large second hand that clicks off the seconds. Stare at it. Notice that some seconds seem longer, or shorter, than others. And if you "play" a little, you may find you can "hold" the second hand in one place for, what would seem to be several seconds.

Tim also had a problem with two clocks. He wanted his marathon clock to read less time than the observed time; he wanted the race to feel more like an hour. One of Tim's downfalls was that he was using his longest run to train for an event that would take more time than the training run itself. In other words, the marathon was even longer than his longest run. Tim had to experience a workout of more than three hours, without overtraining, so the marathon would be relatively shorter. He also had to learn how to manipulate time at will.

Walking was one remedy for both of these time problems. By adding more time to his long run, by walking the first and the last half hour, Tim could increase the total time of his long training session without risking overtraining. Walking also relaxed him in a way running never did.

After two or three of these workouts, Tim learned how easy it was to manipulate time. His total workout of 3.5 hours (a half-hour walk, 2.5 hour run, and a half-hour walk), enabled him to either make the time go faster, or, because he didn't want the now-enjoyable workout to end, go slower. These workouts would re-orient Tim, making the marathon shorter, relative to the long workout. On marathon day, he would be able to make the marathon go by quickly.

This is just what happened, since Tim ran his race in 2 hours and 48 minutes, saying afterwards, "It felt like an easy long run."

These time tactics helped Stu Mittleman attain his world record in the 1,000-Mile Run. This event required a modification of the relationship of time to enable Stu to cope with the 1,000 one-mile laps. Averaging approximately 86 miles a day, Stu successfully manipulated time so that the 11-plus days were psychologically and physiologically less than 11 days. "By the fifth day," Stu recalls, "if you'd ask me how many days went by, I'd say two."

We used these same time games to train Paul Fendler who, in his first-ever ultra-marathon distance, became the Metropolitan Athletic Congress 50-Mile Champion in 1987. "All of a sudden, in the beginning of the race, time ceased to be an existing factor," Fendler recalls, "and it was the walk/run workouts that taught me how to control time."

Einstein thought in holistic terms, and believed that the universe doesn't contain random activity. This certainly includes the organization of the human body and the influence of many factors which affect your training and racing. The aspect of time is merely one of those factors.

26

A Note about Diet and Nutrition

A book on training provides only one aspect of sport. Others include such topics as psychology, aerodynamics, nutrition and diet.

In the case of nutrition and diet, it's not possible to cover that vast topic in one chapter, so I won't attempt to do that. But there are a few points I would like to make on the subject. For more detailed information about diet and nutrition for endurance athletes, refer to *Eating for Endurance*, which I wrote as a companion book to this one.

Most cells of the body have a certain lifespan. For example, your red blood cells live about three months. When they die, some of their parts are recycled. For the most part, however, new materials are formulated to create new red blood cells to replace the ones which are lost. In order to make these new cells, your body uses macro- and micronutrients supplied by foods in your diet.

The macronutrients include the three main building blocks of your physiology: carbohydrates, proteins and fats. The micronutrients are the vitamins, minerals and other elements necessary to regulate macronutrient activity. All these substances provide the body with energy, and new materials to make new cells.

Essentially, the athlete you are this year is different than the athlete you were last year. This is true not only on a biological level — where most of the cells replace themselves — but more so on a molecular level. In this latter case, molecules replace themselves billions at a time with each breath you take in.

If you want to start building a better athlete right now, the quality of the food you consume must be the best you can get — the freshest, least processed, and most natural available.

The phrase, "you are what you eat" can be applied to endurance athletes just as well as anyone else. Consider the very brief introduction to macronutrients given below.

Your energy, whether at rest or during running, comes from the carbohydrates, fats and proteins in your diet. Everyone is uniquely different. The amount of each macronutrient you eat may help or hinder your performance, depending on your specific requirements. Finding your needs should be a priority if you want to improve your overall health and fitness. I never had or will have a particular diet or specific amount of each macronutrient that all athletes should consume. Rather, finding your own optimal needs is what I encourage you to do.

Significant amounts of your energy can come from fats. The more fat you burn, the less you'll store, and the more endurance you'll develop. But for many runners, that four-letter word — fats — has a negative tone. Perhaps it's time to change your attitude about fats.

You have enough stored energy from carbohydrates to get 20 miles into a marathon. If not for fat, it would be impossible to finish the last 10K. And protein can give you an energy bonus of 10 percent. If you optimize your diet, you can have virtually unlimited energy. Let's look at each of the macronutrients and how they could play a role in improving your endurance.

The average person has enough stored fat to run dozens of marathons. This untapped power and endurance source is available, if your body is programmed to use it. But the "low-fat trend," which emphasizes consumption of more carbohydrates and less fats, has only helped many people to turn off their fat-burning potential. Eating some fat can improve your endurance.

In the coming years you'll be hearing more about the merits of fats, and people will discuss the virtues of certain "healthy" or "good" fats. Besides giving us energy, these fats can help fight stress and inflammation, assist your immune system, offer protection from injury and help get calcium into your bones.

The good fats are the ones nature has provided — those from vegetables, nuts, butter, cream, eggs, etc. In a most general sense, it is important to eat more vegetable and other non-animal fats, than saturated animal fats — about twice as much. And remember, butter, eggs and even meats contain some of the monounsaturated fat found in extra-virgin olive oil.

Fats are an essential part of a good diet. No scientist can deny that. We now know that diets that are very low in fat can contribute to heart disease. And the monounsaturated fat found in olive oil helps to prevent breast cancer. For athletes, fats also can help performance.

A diet that's about 25 to 30 percent fat is a reasonable amount when viewing macronutrient intake in this new light. For some athletes, 35 percent or more is necessary for their individual needs, and in others, less. World champion ultramarathoner Stu Mittleman consumes this percentage — or more — when training for his races.

Fats to avoid include the overcooked ones, especially when fried, and hydrogenated fats found in many products. The most common hydrogenated product is margarine. (It's not nice to fool Mother Nature.) Margarine can make your cholesterol picture much worse because it acts even worse than saturated fat once it's in your body. Be sure to read labels on foods you buy in order to avoid these harmful hydrogenated or partially hydrogenated oils. The best rule is, if it's in the list of ingredients, do not put the product in your shopping cart.

But we can't burn fats without carbohydrates. Balance is the key; too much or too little fat or carbohydrate can create problems. In my experience, many people are avoiding too much fat and eating too many carbs. Excess carbohydrates, especially refined ones like white pasta and sugar, can turn off your ability to burn fats.

Consuming carbohydrates stimulates the release of the hormone insulin, which causes a drop in blood sugar. Insulin sends this blood sugar to the cells and increases glycogen storage; essentially it compels your body to use more carbohydrates as fuel. More importantly, insulin converts about 40 percent of your carbohydrates to fat for storage. If you want to use more fats for energy, the insulin response must be moderated. High-glycemic foods such as pasta, cereals, fruit juice and all sugars, results in more insulin being released, more fat stored and less fat burned. The exception to this is during training or competition, when consuming a carbohydrate food or drink will produce little or no insulin. So this discussion of carbohydrates pertains to your meals and snacks.

In many people, excess carbohydrate intake produces excess hunger, moodiness, fatigue, headaches, depression, and other blood-sugar symptoms. Also, sleepiness after meals and intestinal bloating are common symptoms.

If you want to use more fats to fuel your athletic activities and improve endurance, consider moderating (ideally, eliminating) the intake of refined sugars, and keeping all other carbohydrate intake to about 35 to 50 percent of your diet.

Like fat, protein has also been ignored in recent years. The RDA for protein has been revised at least 10 times since 1943, and continues to be a topic for debate. Many feel today's recommendations — 0.8/kg body weight — is too low, with some experts suggesting amounts three to four times the RDA.

Athletes involved in activities which build muscle and endurance, and those subjected to recurring trauma, may need larger protein intakes. Once optimal body size is attained and growth stabilizes, there is still significant and continuous turnover of tissue protein, especially in runners.

The traditional view that higher protein intakes are only required by weight lifters is outdated. Today we know that aerobic endurance training may increase the need for protein even more than anaerobic muscle-building exercise.

Here are some sample meals that are lower in carbohydrate, with 30 percent fat and protein:

- 8 oz. tomato juice, 2 poached eggs on 2 slices of multi-grain toast (dry), ½ cup low-fat cottage cheese.

- Chicken salad with mayo on whole-wheat bread, a mixed salad (lettuce, onions, carrots), extra-virgin olive oil and vinegar.

- Broiled fish, ½ cup brown rice, ½ cup three-bean salad, ½ cup cooked zucchini.

The Athlete's Secret Nutrient

Of all the micro- and macronutrients that are important in overall health and fitness, there is one nutrient even more important. This substance is the most inexpensive and most readily available, but is the most deficient of all nutrients in athletes.

What is this powerful dietary nutrient? Water. Most athletes don't get enough of it during rest, training and racing.

In most endurance events, the majority of competitors finish the race dehydrated. Unfortunately, too many of them start the race the same way. In a 2½-hour endurance event, for example, water loss may reduce water content in the body by up to 10 percent, despite efforts to drink enough water. This is a significant and dangerous situation which affects both your health and performance.

Of all the nutritional needs, water is the most important. It is second only to oxygen in its importance to your body. About 60 percent or more of a male athlete's weight is water, slightly less for females. Normally, about two-thirds of your water supply comes from drinking fluids (mostly water). About one third comes from foods (about 10 percent is produced by your cells during the conversion of carbohydrates and fats to energy).

Water input must balance water loss, both at rest and during exercise. Water loss occurs from several areas of the body. Evaporation of water from the skin is important to control body temperature. Surprisingly, about 30 percent of your water loss occurs under cool, resting conditions. But during endurance activity, sweating increases this amount dramatically — about 300 times the amount lost during rest! The amount is determined in part by air temperature and body size. The higher the temperature or larger the body size, the greater the water loss.

Water lost through exhaled air is also significant. The air going into and out of your lungs needs to be humidified. Due to the increased breathing rate during exercise and racing, this amount of water loss is increased five to 10 times.

Most of the water lost during rest occurs through the kidneys. This water is used to help eliminate waste products from the body. But during exercise, the body attempts to conserve water, and loss through the kidneys is very limited — 50 to 70 times less than when at rest. And small but significant water loss (about 5 percent) is through the intestine at rest. Unless an athlete has diarrhea during an event, there is no water loss from the intestine during exercise or competition.

One of the biggest problems of dehydration is that it decreases blood volume. Maintaining blood volume is important because of so many vital functions associated with it:

- Red blood cells carry oxygen to the muscles via blood.

- Nutrients, including glucose, fats and amino acids, are transported in the blood.

- Through the blood, carbon dioxide and other waste products are removed.

- Hormones that regulate muscular activity during exercise (and aid in recovery) are carried by the blood.

- The blood neutralizes lactic acid to maintain the proper pH.

- Water removes excess heat generated during exercise via the blood.

- Blood volume helps maintain efficient cardiovascular function.

Water loss also reduces the athlete's performance potential, sometimes dramatically. Even minimal amounts of water loss impair performance. Studies show that even in short events, dehydration is significant. For example, an athlete who can run a 10,000-meter race in 35 minutes when normally hydrated, will take almost 38 minutes when dehydrated by 4 percent. An athlete who is well hydrated performing at 100 percent will diminish performance by 10 percent if he or she is only 2 percent dehydrated. If 5 percent dehydrated, the athlete's performance will diminish by 30 percent. This latter example can mean an extra 3 hours or more in an Ironman race!

In conjunction with performance changes with dehydration come higher heart rates. Four hours of training without water may cause the heart rate to increase by 30 beats.

Comparing the total water loss during rest to competition, water needs increase 10-15 times. In races such as the Japan Ironman, the amount of water lost by an average individual can be as much as 1.5 to 2.5 liters per hour!

It's obvious that water needs increase during exercise and especially with competition. But how can you compensate for such dramatic losses in water, especially during competition?

The sensation of thirst, regulated by the area of the brain called the hypothalmus, occurs due to the lower concentration of water in the blood. So when you feel thirsty, you're already dehydrated. With most athletes, this delays the intake of water. Following heavy sweating, complete water replacement may take 24 to 48 hours. So thirst is not a good indication that you need water because that need exists long before you feel thirsty. Unfortunately, the human body does not function like many other animals (by drinking enough water they can consume 10 percent of their total body weight within the first few minutes after heavy exercise). Humans need to frequently drink water in smaller amounts.

The best way to regulate water levels is to drink plain water all day long. Avoid carbonated water as it may cause intestinal distress. And during training and competition, the same is true; smaller amounts on a regular basis throughout the activity is the best way to stay hydrated. Despite this, most competitors will cross the finish line dehydrated to some degree. In addition to not being able to replenish water fast enough, most athletes physically cannot consume enough water. Forcing water beyond your ability will only result in stomach bloating (from swallowing air) or nausea.

During endurance events, liquids containing carbohydrates and sodium are of great value. But these should be in addition to plain water taken during the event. Consuming carbohydrate is important for immediate energy and to maintain the burning of fats — your most important endurance fuel.

Sodium deficiency is related to dehydration and is a major concern in endurance activity. With dehydration comes more than just water deficiency. As exercise intensity and duration increase, the sweating rate also increases and sodium loss is accelerated, with minimal losses of potassium. Low blood sodium, called hyponatremia, can result in general weakness and disorientation, and in extreme cases seizures and coma.

In long events, like an Ironman event, too much water intake without sodium may aggravate sodium deficiency. So in those events, taking sodium can be very helpful. That's why many sports drinks contain sodium.

Since the body uses water to dissipate heat, the risk of heat illness goes hand in hand with dehydration and sodium loss. Even short races in hot weather can cause heat illness. With heat illness, three stages are seen: muscle cramps, exhaustion and heat stroke.

Muscle cramping, sometimes quite severe, is a classic end result of dehydration. It first attacks the larger, most often used muscles such as the hamstring and quadriceps group, and the calf muscles. Some of the cramping may also be due to sodium deficiency.

The second stage of heat exhaustion is first accompanied by excess fatigue, dizziness and shortness of breath. Later symptoms include vomiting and fainting. Dehydration causes the cardiovascular system to become inefficient. During this stage of heat illness, blood flow to both the muscles and skin is diminished; the muscles become deficient in nutrients and body heat accumulates.

The last stage of heat illness is heat stroke. This is a life-threatening disorder that requires immediate medical attention. The signs include a high internal body temperature (40 degrees C), cessation of sweating, very rapid pulse and breathing, hot and dry skin, confusion and often unconsciousness. If unattended, heat stroke can progress to coma and death. First-aid treatment includes cooling the body with cold water or ice.

What should you do to prevent dehydration? Here are some general everyday guidelines:

- Don't wait for a race to start hydrating. Drink water everyday, throughout the day, especially the week before an event. Drink smaller amounts all day, rather than two or three large doses.

- Have a water bottle near you at all times, and get into the habit of drinking water. Especially keep water near your immediate area during work hours (at your desk, by the phone, etc.) or where you spend much of your time.

- Consume sodium-rich foods (vegetables, sea salt and soy sauce) regularly, especially during hot weather and the week before an event.

- Get used to drinking water before, during and immediately after training. Simulate race conditions to practice drinking water at faster paces. Learn to drink without swallowing air.

- Discover which drinks (those with carbohydrates and sodium) make you feel the best and are well tolerated. Experiment during training rather than during a race.

27

The Full Spectrum of Drug Use

Drugs have been used to improve athletic performance for thousands of years. More recently, those who recall the movie "Damn Yankees" know the human-nature story about selling your soul to the devil for one short-lived, but great, performance. But the drug problem in all sports is still fact, not fiction. This is especially true when we consider the big picture of drug use — from the social-legal drugs, to the illegal ones, and those natural versions of performance-enhancing drugs. This also includes the use of drugs both on and off the course.

A variety of drugs and natural substances, whether illicit, prescription, over-the-counter, natural or synthetic, may or may not help an individual attain higher levels of endurance performance. In many cases, the physiological benefits differ from the psychological ones, as the placebo effect is very much a part of the drug culture. The fact is, any athlete can get there just fine, thank you, legally, and healthfully, without the use of illegal erythropoietin, legal aspirin and other drugs. At least this is true in endurance sports, as these champions develop themselves through proper training and lifestyle, while sprinters are born with significant genetic talent. Those who seek a natural route to optimal performance in the endurance arena will also enjoy a longer athletic life.

The intrigue and misuse of drugs to enhance performance, when effective, often results in a "one-shot" great race effort. These athletes often are never heard from again. This single great race pattern also exists in overtrained athletes and, interestingly, may be associated with dramatic but temporary excessive increases in natural hormones. Compare this with the performances of great natural athletes, like six-time Hawaii Ironman Triathlon Champion Mark Allen, who over the course of many years consistently performed to his potential.

Many athletes will say they never have, and never would, use drugs. But let's face it, most of us — almost all athletes at every level — take drugs. Consider your addiction to caffeine, your use of aspirin or other non-steroidal anti-inflammatory drugs (NSAIDs), or even alcohol (the last two, when combined even in moderate amounts, may cause liver damage). Looking at this full spectrum of drug use is an important social perspective of this common problem.

When the issue of drugs comes up, most don't think of this full spectrum of drug use. But when illicit drugs are discussed, there's almost always a negative connotation. So is the problem the legality issue? A drug's potential effect on health? The issue of its unfair advantage over athletes who don't take drugs? Clearly, it's an issue of all of these factors, and others as well.

There are a variety of issues associated with drug use: legal, ethical and health issues are among them. In these discussions, we must differentiate between illegal drug use, banned substances, prescription drugs, over-the-counter drugs, and so-called natural remedies that stimulate hormone production, or the natural hormones themselves. This complex subject includes diverse opinions from many professionals, lawmakers and athletes, but there are some relatively simple answers.

Social-Legal Drugs

Many drugs commonly consumed with the intention of increasing sports performance are so-called social-legal drugs like caffeine, aspirin and other NSAIDs, and alcohol. Perhaps it's their legal use (except for underage drinkers), or easy availability that makes them so popular.

Caffeine

Can't get to your morning workout without coffee? Some people are clearly addicted to caffeine, and in some cases rely on this natural drug in order to perform. Caffeine has a definite effect on increasing performance in mild and moderate amounts (higher levels don't further increase performance as many think). And for many people, even moderate amounts of caffeine are not unhealthy. However, many can tolerate small to moderate amounts of caffeine in substances like coffee and tea. Like everything else, this issue is very individual. But consider the facts.

The performance effect of caffeine is linked to its increased fat-burning effect, and sparing of glycogen. This effect can also be achieved naturally through proper training and diet. The effects of caffeine are present with urinary caffeine levels that are below the limit of 12 micrograms/ml allowed by the International Olympic Committee. Caffeine reaches its peak effect about an hour after consumption. For those engaged in longer training or racing, the withdrawal effect that occurs after this peak may leave you hanging midway through your effort.

Too much caffeine, defined differently for each person, can counteract performance as well. The most significant problem is dehydration, as caffeine is a diuretic. These effects can be further amplified in hot weather and at altitude. Calcium and magnesium loss may also be increased in those who consume caffeine, affecting muscle contraction. Immune function may also be adversely effected by caffeine intake, a problem that many athletes have anyway.

Some athletes drink caffeine because of fatigue. Finding the cause of this reduced energy (and sometimes lowered initiative) and correcting it will eliminate the "need" for caffeine. In addition, with use over a long period of time, caffeine may adversely affect bone metabolism.

Aspirin and Other NSAIDs

Many athletes are frequently injured and often rely heavily on NSAIDs to control symptoms, and indirectly, to control performance. These substances are the most commonly recommended and prescribed drugs in the world. While their use may not correct a particular injury, it often decreases discomfort or pain, and allows the continuation of training and racing (which can further worsen the problem). While over-the-counter doses of NSAIDs generally can reduce pain, they don't have much anti-inflammatory effect compared to prescription items.

The potential danger from the continued use of aspirin and other NSAIDs can be extensive. The side effects range from muscle dysfunction and exercise-associated muscle damage, to impaired cartilage repair, impaired fracture healing, and suppression of melatonin and disturbances in sleep patterns. NSAIDs also come with the side effect of intestinal bleeding, which occurs most of the time, with the risk of ulcers.

In high doses, NSAIDs' effect of reducing inflammation occurs from its influence on eicosanoid metabolism. It's possible to achieve the same effects through properly balancing the fats in your diet. For example, increasing your omega-3 fats (fish or linseed oil) may help balance your eicosanoids, allowing your body to produce its own anti-inflammatory chemicals (See *Eating for Endurance*). In doing so, you'll improve your recovery from training and racing.

Alcohol

Mild to moderate consumption of alcohol has numerous positive and negative attributes. But beyond these amounts, high intakes of alcohol are problematic. More significant may be the reasons athletes drink alcohol to excess. Alcohol consumption is higher in athletes than non-athletes, perhaps due to pain, depression or the frustration of sport.

Alcohol suppresses pain, and some athletes know this very well. But too much also can interfere with the body's production of anti-inflammatory chemicals, and can increase free radicals (other chemicals that can damage muscles and other tissue). Both of these effects can contribute to pain. Too much alcohol may also reduce fat-burning ability, which will interfere with endurance. In addition, too much alcohol can increase the need for a variety of nutrients, including vitamin B1, niacin, folic acid and zinc. Deficiencies in these nutrients can in turn impair performance.

Illegal Drugs

Both adults and adolescents have been known to take illegal drugs in an attempt to improve performance. Perhaps the biggest problem is in power sports, including those endurance athletes who casually enter that arena just to work out (and are heavily influenced by power athletes and coaches). In this population, androgenic-anabolic compounds — anabolic steroids — are the misused drug of choice.

Anabolic steroids mimic male sex hormones, or androgens, such as testosterone, increasing skeletal muscle growth. "Designer" synthetic steroids can now work more on building muscle and less on the masculinizing effects. In addition to helping build muscle mass, these steroids may speed recovery (so athletes can train harder and more often).

Prevalence rates for steroid use may be between 5 and 15 percent. Steroid users generally are more likely to be men and boys, participate in strength-related sports, and may use other illicit drugs. Herein lies an important issue: drug use in sports may have association with other social and psychological make-ups. Moreover, if their availability were increased, probably more of these drugs would be used.

Synthetic growth hormone is also used in a similar way to promote muscle growth and recovery. This hormone is often used with anabolic steroids. The body normally produces natural growth hormone in response to training. Diets containing adequate fat can improve the natural response of growth hormone to exercise.

Erythropoietin

This hormone, normally produced by the kidneys, stimulates the production of red blood cells. These cells carry oxygen to your muscles and are directly related to endurance performance, as increasing the number of red blood cells (and hemoglobin) can improve performance. This was the original idea, dating back perhaps to the mid-1970s, behind a technique called red-blood-cell infusion, or "blood doping." In this approach, the athlete has blood removed and stored for one to two months. During this time, the body compensates and makes more red blood cells. Within a week before competition, the blood is re-infused, and the athlete now has much more red blood cells and hemoglobin, which can help performance.

In recent years, erythropoietin is being illegally injected to get the same effect without having to remove blood. Unfortunately, testing athletes for increased presence of erythropoietin, along with testosterone and growth hormone, is more difficult since these hormones are also produced normally by the body (although not at such high levels). Through the use of a hypobaric chamber, Epo can be stimulated in a natural way, both legally and healthily.

One factor forgotten in all this drug talk is the psychological stress created as a result of taking illicit drugs or performing illegal procedures. Associated with this stress may be the desperation or emotional misgiving felt by the athlete. The guilt, secrecy, lying and other activities connected with taking drugs can produce significant stress, further reducing performance capability. (Of course, some athletes feel no guilt about cheating.) Whatever the end-result stress, it further has an adverse effect on the hormones. For example, increased stress elevates the hormone cortisol, which can reduce DHEA and testosterone.

Natural Stimulation

A recent Russian medical journal stated, "the use of strongly active drugs is not necessary because a large reserve is available of drugs of plant and animal origin possessing much lesser side effects." Does the use of a more natural substance from plants, for example, make their use legal, ethical or healthy? The legal issue is most clear — a positive drug test can get you in trouble as an athlete. The question of ethics and health are tied together. If there is a need to increase a certain hormone, i.e., an athlete has abnormally reduced levels, such as testosterone, it would be unethical and unhealthy to avoid correcting the problem. But pumping testosterone or any other hormone up to very high levels with so-called natural hormones available over-the-counter may not only be unhealthy, but unethical and sometimes illegal.

Unfortunately, many endurance athletes use such over-the-counter natural products as DHEA, pregnenolone and melatonin, which can increase the production of testosterone and other substances which can improve performance. The fact is, these substances can be harmful when used improperly, despite the fact that their use can be helpful in specific situations.

Testosterone

Natural testosterone strengthens bones and muscles, aids in recovery from training and racing, and increases sexual desire. Therefore, if you have a history of stress fractures, poor recovery from training or racing, or reduced sex drive, it may be indicative of low levels of testosterone. A simple test, such as a salivary hormone assessment, can determine your levels of this and other hormones. In addition, the use of the antibiotic tetracycline reduces testosterone, as can low-fat and low-cholesterol diets (testosterone and other steroid hormones are synthesized from cholesterol). Overtraining ultimately results in low testosterone levels, often significantly, and may serve, along with other hormones such as cortisol, as a marker of overtraining. Low testosterone levels are often secondary to lowered DHEA.

Dehydroepiandrosterone (DHEA)

In the body, significant amounts of testosterone can come from DHEA. This hormone is often reduced during any type of stress, including hard training and overtraining, and during middle age. Low DHEA is often associated with and primary to low estrogen in women. Those who have difficulty maintaining normal levels of sodium and water during longer training and racing may have low DHEA levels.

Since DHEA can increase estrogen in women, and testosterone in men, it may be contraindicated if you have or are at risk for conditions associated with excess estrogen, such as breast cancer or endometriosis, or conditions associated with excess testosterone, such as prostate cancer. Long-term supplementation with DHEA may also cause your adrenal glands to produce less of its own DHEA, making you dependent upon supplements. If all this sounds too complicated, it's not. Measuring your hormones is easy and reliable as discussed below.

Doses of 5 mg of DHEA are often effective therapeutically, and amounts as high as 50 mg may not be detected in the urine with drug tests. Higher doses are detectable but usually only within 8 hours of taking DHEA.

Other Natural Products

A variety of over-the-counter natural substances can affect hormone production. For example, melatonin can stimulate growth hormone, and natural progesterone can produce testosterone.

Ephedrine, a nervous-system stimulant, is another natural substance used in the sports arena. This relatively mild drug is sometimes used to treat moderate attacks of bronchial asthma and to relieve nasal congestion. However, athletes may become dependent on ephedrine. It may improve performance (especially when combined with caffeine), and may increase fat-burning — a common reason many use it. Ephedrine is a banned substance by the IOC, and is sometimes found in herbal remedies. Its use is commonly associated with athletes who have eating disorders. Like other stimulants, it can be addictive and unhealthy.

Non-Chemical Enhancers

Both mild hyperbaric chambers and hypobaric chambers may benefit athletes and improve performance — sometimes significantly. Athletes may spend an hour or so at rest in a mild hyperbaric chamber to increase oxygen uptake. Similarly, spending time during the day or evening, or even sleeping for a night in a hypobaric chamber can increase the kidney's natural production of natural erythropoietin.

Assessing the Need

What will help you reach your potential without sacrificing your health? The answer to that important question comes from the assessment process. It will require work on your part, often with the help of the right professional. If, for example, your iron levels are low, or your hemoglobin is low, you may have reduced endurance performance. Or, if your body's DHEA or testosterone level is low, the same reduced performance might be expected. Eating foods high in iron, or careful supplementation of this mineral, or taking a DHEA supplement, could significantly improve not only your performance but your overall health as well. These and other vital pieces of information can be attained easily through proper dietary evaluation (see *Eating for Endurance*), and your hormone levels may be assessed through salivary hormone tests.

Whether it's a hormone, vitamin, mineral, or other type of supplement, finding out if you have a need for a particular substance that may enhance performance is the first step to reaching your potential. As obvious as that may sound, most athletes skip the evaluation step and take what other athletes are taking. But most supplements work only when the need for them exists — taking more iron pills when your body does not require more will not give added benefits, and often may cause harm. If DHEA levels are normal, more won't necessarily help, and can often hurt. However, if there's a need for more iron, more DHEA, or any substance that is too low, providing that substance can improve endurance.

Perhaps the single, most obvious answer to the drug question is whether you need help in balancing your fitness and health beyond your normal training and dietary habits. If this is the case, these improvements can most often be attained naturally. Synthetic drugs may sometimes temporarily boost your fitness, but at the same time can impair your health. A balanced athlete will naturally develop his or her endurance and achieve optimal performance capability, not just for the next race but for life.

The suspicion of drug use is much more common than its use. And this problem — the perception of misuse — can sometimes prevent other athletes from having great aspirations in their sport. Cynically, some even insist that the great performances are drug-induced. Unfortunately, that is sometimes the case, as has been documented in the world of track and field and bicycle racing. There have been a few positive drug tests in triathlon — which have been vociferously disputed. Likely, there have been a few cases that have gone undetected. But it need not be. From my experiences of working with drug-free professional triathletes like Mark Allen and Mike Pigg, and more importantly many age groupers (some of whom began as couch potatoes), it's quite clear that a drug-free effort will result in great fitness and health benefits for many years, and can propel an athlete to the absolute pinnacle of any sport.

28

U.S. Athletes: Fit but Unhealthy?

The Games of the XXIV Olympiad in Seoul, South Korea, in 1988 provided me with a first-hand look at the world's great athletes. I also witnessed the continued decline of American athletes.

In 1896, Greece dominated the first Olympic Games by winning the most medals — 47 — but in Seoul, Greece managed but a single one. As so often happens in sport, the winners have no place to go but down, as "the losers now will be later to win." Bob Dylan's words have echoed over America for the last couple of decades, and so too have the former foreign losers been winning over American athletes.

The steady decline of American athletic dominance has been slow enough that hardly anyone seems to be noticing, except for the rest of the world. The Soviets, Chinese and Germans, for example, are among many countries who have progressively developed more and more champions. This is not to say that American athletes have not been progressing among themselves. Although they may still break their own records, American athletes have not kept pace with the rest of the world.

When Bryant Gumbel told a world television audience that the U.S. athletes were not as good as the '84 team, and not as talented as the Soviets, NBC boldly predicted the obvious. By noon Sunday, the first medals were presented: gold and bronze to the Soviets, and silver to the East Germans. The stage was now set, and the Games continued with that same pace. These Olympics would be the worst showing in history for the United States.

The glaring problem plaguing U.S. athletes is their lack of health inside otherwise fit bodies. This fitness/health imbalance is so common it's often thought to be a normal aspect of athletics. Unfortunately, it prevents some of our best performers from ever reaching the Games while other countries more often send their best.

How do we define fitness and health? Fitness infers athletic ability. The first place finisher is more fit than the runner-up. Health is a state where all the systems of the body — digestive, nervous, circulatory, hormonal, etc. — are working optimally. American athletes are knowingly and unknowingly sacrificing health for more fitness. Too often they are injured, ill and occasionally even die in the course of their active careers. Both fitness and health should be balanced. The causes are many: diet and nutritional imbalances, overtraining, improper care and even attitude.

Attitude problems are more common in U.S. athletes. Some hope and believe that a lot of luck, or "waking up on the right side of the bed," as silver medalist Michelle Mitchell said, will produce a gold medal. This creates overwhelming stress from competition unlike that seen in most foreign athletes. "Competition makes me happy," said Chinese diver Xu Yanmei, after beating Mitchell for the gold.

This excess competitive stress can, in an unhealthy athlete, cause harm before and during competition, and can affect the results. In the previous winter Olympic Games in Calgary, Canada, U.S. skater Debi Thomas' unsuccessful bid for a gold is one such example. Thomas was unable to perform even near her best due to stress, losing a seemingly easy gold medal. And in Seoul, many foreign swimmers performed a personal best, while most Americans left theirs at the trials weeks earlier.

U.S. athletes and coaches, in their search for the reasons foreign athletes are over-running international events, often cite drugs, the "professional athlete" issue, and money problems as causes for the U.S. decline. But our athletes are as capable as any population in the world, and have as much opportunity, if not more, than anyone. The financial concern was best exemplified in the Calgary Games: The U.S. ski team spent $21 million without producing a final-round qualifier, whereas all the medal winning countries combined spent less money.

A more serious money problem, one which affects the health of our future Olympians, comes from the very companies who are "official" sponsors of the U.S. Olympic Team. Many of these companies sell unhealthy products, such as candy bars, colas and alcohol, and spend many millions to advertise their products to, among others, young Olympic hopefuls. And even though the U.S. Olympic Committee does not endorse these products as healthy, our nation's young are more naive and view these products as "foods of champions."

Our dwindling number of champions is the result of numerous other factors as well. Perhaps the most damaging one is the emphasis of "no pain, no gain." This insistence on quantity, where more is thought to be better, rather than quality, in which both health and fitness are considered, has unfortunately been a mainstream of American sports for decades.

With an emphasis on building health, and not just bodies, American athletes could minimize injuries, increase their careers and perform at higher levels. As much as any American, I would like to see our athletes perform as they should — "as good as gold." We can begin re-establishing our athletic dominance the next Olympics. However, this will not happen until we put aside our strong traditional unhealthy trends.

The unwillingness of many to break this tradition is another problem, as more and more countries progress farther ahead of the U.S. in many training and therapeutic abilities. It may be the Asians, led by Japan, China and Korea, who will be the dominant athletic force of the near future, as "the times they are a-changin."

References

Abernethy PJ, Thayer R, Taylor AW (1990). Acute and chronic responses of skeletal muscle to endurance and sprint exercise. *A review. Sports Med.* 10(6): 365-389.

Adlercreutz H, Harkonen M, Kuoppasalmi K, Naveri H, Huhtaniemi I, Tikkanen H, Remes K, Dessypris A, Karvonen J (1986). Effect of training on plasma anabolic and catabolic steroid hormones and their response during physical exercise. *Int. J. Sports Med.* 7: 27-28.

Ahmaidi S, Granier P, Taoutaou Z, Mercier J, Dubouchaud H, Prefaut C (1996). Effects of active recovery on plasma lactate and anaerobic power following repeated intensive exercise. *Med. Sci. Sports Exerc.* 28(4): 450-456.

Arena B, Maffulli N, Maffulli F, Morleo MA (1995). Reproductive hormones and menstrual changes with exercise in female athletes. *Sports Med.* 19(4): 278-287.

Bale P, Doust J, Dawson D (1996). Gymnasts, distance runners, anorexics body composition and menstrual status. *J. Sports Med. Phys. Fitness* 36(1): 49-53.

Barrett J, Bilisko T (1995). The role of shoes in the prevention of ankle sprains. *Sports Med.* 20(4): 277-280.

Basmajian JV, Bentzon JW (1954). An electromyographic study of certain muscles of the leg and foot in the standing position. *Surg. Gynecol. Obstet.* 98: 662-666. Abstr.

Bell GJ, Petersen SR, Wessel J, Bagnall K, Quinney HA (1991). Physiological adaptations to concurrent endurance training and low velocity resistance training. *Int. J. Sports Med.* 12(4): 384-390.

Benson JE, Engelbert-Fenton KA, Eisenman PA (1996). Nutritional aspects of amenorrhea in the female athlete triad. *Int. J. Sport Nutr.* 6(2): 134-145.

Bogdanis GC, Nevill ME, Lakomy HK, Graham CM, Louis G (1996). Effects of active recovery on power output during repeated maximal sprint cycling. *Eur. J. Appl. Physiol.* 74(5): 461-469.

Butterfield GE (1999). Nutrient requirements at high altitude. *Clin Sports Med*;18(3):607-21.

Cahan C, et al. (1990). Assessing the characteristic between length of hypoxic exposure and serum erythropoietin levels. *Am J Physiol*; 258(4 Pt 2):R1016-1021.

Chao WH, et al. (1999). Oxidative stress in humans during work at moderate altitude. *J Nutr*;129(11):2009-12.

Colliander EB, Dudley GA, Tesch PA (1988). Skeletal muscle fiber type composition and performance during repeated bouts of maximal, concentric contractions. *Eur. J. Appl. Physiol.* 58: 81-86.

Costill DL, Flynn MG, Kirwan JP, Houmard JA, Mitchell JB, Thomas R (1988). Effects of repeated days of intensified training on muscle glycogen and swimming performance. *Med. Sci. Sports Exerc.* 20: 249-254.

Coyle EF, Sidossis LS, Horowitz JF, Beltz JD (1992). Cycling efficiency is related to the percentage of type I muscle fibers. *Med. Sci. Sports Exerc.* 24(7):782-788.

Ding JH, Sheckter CB, Drinkwater BL, Soules MR, Bremner WJ (1988). High serum cortisol levels in exercise-associated amenorrhea. *Ann. Intern. Med.* 108(4): 530-534.

Dueck CA, Matt KS, Manore MM, Skinner JS (1996). Treatment of athletic amenorrhea with a diet and training intervention program. *Int. J. Sport Nutr.* 6(1): 24-40.

Eckardt KU, et al. (1989). Rate of erythropoietin formation in humans in response to acute hypobaric hypoxia. *J Appl Physiol*;66(4):1785-1788.

Fry RW, Morton AR, Garcia-Webb P, Crawford, GPM, Keast D (1992). Biological responses to overload training in endurance sports. *Eur. J. Appl. Physiol.* 64: 335-344.

Fry RW, Morton AR, Keast D (1991). Overtraining in athletes, an update. *Sports Med.* 12(1): 32-65.

REFERENCES

Gardner LI Jr, Dziados JE, Jones BH, Brundage JF, Harris JM, Sullivan R, Gill P (1988). Prevention of lower extremity stress fractures: a controlled trial of a shock absorbent insole. *Am. J. Public Health* 78(12): 1563-1567.

Grace TG, Skipper BJ, Newberry JC, Nelson MA, Sweetser ER, Rothman ML (1988). Prophylactic knee braces and injury to the lower extremity. *J. Bone Joint Surg.* 70(3): 422-427.

Graves JE, Martin AD, Miltenberger LA, Pollock ML (1988). Physiological responses to walking with hand weights, wrist weights, and ankle weights. *Med. Sci. Sports Exerc.* 20(3): 265-271.

Guezennec CY, et al. (1989). Influence of polyunsaturated fatty acid diet on the hemorrheological response to physical exercise in hypoxia. *Int J Sports Med*;10(4):286-91.

Hakkinen K, Pakarinen A, Alen M, Komi PV (1985). Serum hormones during prolonged training of neuromuscular performance. *Eur. J. Appl. Physiol.* 53(4): 287-293.

Hodgetts V, Coppack SW, Frayn KN, Hockadag DR (1991). Factors controlling fat mobilization from human subcutaneous adipose tissue during exercise *J. Appl. Physiol.* 71: 445-451.

Horne L, Bell G, Fisher B, Warren S, Janowska-Wieczorek A (1997). Interaction between cortisol and tumour necrosis factor with concurrent resistance and endurance training. *Clin. J. Sport Med.* 7(4): 247-251.

Horowitz JF, Sidossis LS, Coyle EF (1994). High efficiency of type I muscle fibers improves performance. *Int. J. Sports Med.* 15(3): 152-157.

Johnson WG, Carr-Nangle RE, Bergeron KC (1995). Macronutrient intake, eating habits, and exercise as moderators of menstrual distress in healthy women. *Psychosom. Med.* 57(4): 324-330.

Jones BH, Cowan DN, Knapik JJ (1994). Exercise, training and injuries. *Sports Med.* 18(3): 202-214.

Jones BH, Cowan DN, Tomlinson JP, Robinson JR, Polly DW, Frykman PN (1993). Epidemiology of injuries associated with physical training among young men in the army. *Med. Sci. Sports Exerc.* 25(2): 197-203.

Jorgensen U (1990). Body load in heel-strike running: the effect of a firm heel counter. *Am. J. Sports Med.* 18(2): 177-181.

Krivickas LS (1997). Anatomical factors associated with overuse sports injuries. *Sports Med.* 24(2): 132-146.

Kuipers H (1994). Exercise-induced muscle damage. *Int. J. Sports Med.* 15(3): 132-135.

Kuipers H, Keizer HA (1988). Overtraining in elite athletes: Review and directions for the future. *Sports Medicine* 6: 79-92.

Laughlin GA, Dominguez CE, Yen SS (1998). Nutritional and endocrine-metabolic aberrations in women with functional hypothalamic amenorrhea. *J. Clin. Endocrinol. Metab.* 83(1): 25-32.

Leaf DA, Kleinman MT, Hamilton M, Barstow TJ (1997). The effect of exercise intensity on lipid peroxidation. *Med. Sci. Sports Exerc.* 29(8): 1036-1039.

Lehmann MJ, Lormes W, Opitz-Gress A, Steinacher JM, Netzer N, Foster C, Gastmann U (1997). Training and overtraining: an overview and experimental results in endurance sports. *J. Sports Med. Phys. Fitness* 37: 7-17.

McCarthy JP, Agre JC, Graf BK, Pozniak MA, Vailas AC (1995). Compatibility of adaptive responses with combining strength and endurance training. *Med. Sci. Sports Exerc.* 27(3): 429-436.

Newsholme EA (1994). Biochemical mechanisms to explain immunosuppression in well-trained and overtrained athletes. *Int. J. Sports Med.* 15: 142-147.

Moquin A, Mazzeo, R. (2000). Effect of mild dehydration on the lactate threshold in women. *Med. Sci. Sports Exerc.*, Vol. 32, No. 2, pp. 396-402.

O'Connor PJ, Morgan WP, Raglin JS, Barksdale CM, Kalin NH (1989). Mood state and salivary cortisol levels following overtraining in female swimmers. *Psychoneuroendocrinology* 14(4): 303-310.

Pellise F, Navarro-Quilis A (1997). The muscles in chronic ligamentous instability of the knee: an experimental study. *Acta. Orthop. Belg.* 63(4): 287-293. Abstr.

Perlman M, Leveille D, DeLeonibus J (1987). Inversion lateral ankle trauma: differential diagnosis, review of literature, and prospective studies. *J. Foot. Surg.* 26: 95-135.

Pronai W, et al. (1995). Folic acid supplementation improves erythropoietin response. *Nephron*;71(4):395-400.

Rawal SB, et al. (1999). Effect of time exposure to high altitude on zinc and copper concentrations in human plasma. *Aviat Space Environ Med*;70(12):1161-5.

Richalet JP, et al. (1992). Use of a hypobaric chamber for pre-acclimatization before climbing Mount Everest. *Int J Sports Med*;13 Suppl 1:S216-20.

Robbins S, Hanna AM (1987). Running-related injury prevention through barefoot adaptations. *Med. Sci. Sports Exerc.* 19(2): 148-156.

Robbins S, Waked E (1997a). Balance and vertical impact in sports: role of shoe sole materials. *Arch. Phys. Med. Rehabil.* 78(5): 463-467.

Robbins S, Waked E (1997b). Hazard of deceptive advertising of athletic footwear. *Br. J. Sports Med.* 31(4): 299-303.

Robbins S, Waked E (1998). Factors associated with ankle injuries. *Sports Med.* 25(1): 63-72.

Robbins S, Waked E, Gouw GJ, McClaran J (1994). Athletic footwear affects balance in men. *Br. J. Sports Med.* 28(2): 117-122.

Robbins S, Waked E, McClaran J (1995). Proprioception and stability: foot position awareness as a function of age and footwear. *Age Ageing* 24(1): 67-72.

Robbins S, Waked E, Rappel R (1995). Ankle taping improves proprioception before and after exercise in young men. *Br. J. Sports Med.* 29(4): 242-247.

Roberts AC, McClure RD, Weiner RI, Brooks GA (1993). Overtraining affects male reproductive status. *Fertil. Steril.*60(4): 686-692.

Rodriguez, F. et al. (1999). Intermittent hypobaric hypoxia stimulates erythropoiesis and improves aerobic capacity. *Med Sci Sports Exerc;* 31(2): 264-268.

Rovere GD, Clarke TJ, Yates CS, Burley K (1988). Retrospective comparison of taping and ankle stabilizers in preventing ankle injuries. *Am. J. Sports Med.* 16(3): 228-233.

Rovere GD, Haupt HA, Yates CS (1987). Prophylactic knee bracing in college football. *Am. J. Sports Med.* 15(2): 111-116.

Safran MR, Garrett WE, Seaber AV, Glisson RR, Ribbeck BM (1988). The role of warmup in muscular injury prevention. *Am. J. Sports Med.* 16(2): 123-129.

Safran MR, Seaber AV, Garrett WE Jr (1989). Warm-up and muscular injury prevention. An update. *Sports Med.* 8(4): 239-249.

Shellock FG, Prentice WE (1985). Warming-up and stretching for improved physical performance and prevention of sports-related injuries. *Sports Med.* 2(4): 267-278.

Simoneau JA, Lortie G, Boulay MR, Marcotte M, Thibault MC, Bouchard C (1985). Human skeletal muscle fiber type alteration with high-intensity intermittent training. *Eur. J. Appl. Physiol.* 54: 250-253.

Skinner HB, Wyatt MP, Stone ML, Hodgdon JA, Barrack RL (1986). Exercise-related knee joint laxity. *Am. J. Sports Med.* 14(1): 30-34.

Smith LL et al.(1993). The effects of static and ballistic stretching on delayed onset muscle soreness and creatine kinase. *Res. Q. Exerc. Sport* 64(1): 103-107.

Snyder AC, Kuipers H, Cheng B, Servais R, Fransen E (1995). Overtraining following intensified training with normal muscle glycogen. *Med. Sci. Sports Exerc.* 27: 1063-1070.

Stone MH, Keith RE, Kearney JT (1991). Overtraining: a review of the signs, symptoms and possible causes. *J. Appl. Sports Sci. Res.* 5(1): 35-50.

Taoutaou Z, Granier P, Mercier B, Mercier J, Ahmaidi S, Prefaut C (1996). Lactate kinetics during passive and partially active recovery in endurance and sprint athletes. *Eur. J. Appl. Physiol.* 73(5): 465-470.

Teitz CC, Hermanson BK, Kronmal RA, Diehr PH (1987). Evaluation of the use of braces to prevent injury to the knee in collegiate football players. *J. Bone Joint Surg.* 69(1): 2-9.

Thonnard JL, Bragard D, Willems PA (1996). Stability of the braced ankle: a biomechanical investigation. *Am. J. Sports Med.* 24: 356-361.

Tomaro J, Burdett RG (1993). The effects of foot orthotics on the EMG activity of selected leg muscles during gait. *J. Orthop. Sports Phys. Ther.* 18(4): 532-536.

Urhausen A, Gabriel H, Kindermann W (1997). Blood hormones as markers of training stress and overtraining. *Sports Med.* 20(4): 251-276.

Van Mechelen W, Hlobil H, Kemper HC, Voorn WJ (1983). Prevention of running injuries by warm-up, cool-down, and stretching exercises. *Am. J. Sports Med.* 21(5): 711-719.

Weidner TG, Gehlsen G, Schurr T, Dwyer GB (1997). Effects of viral upper respiratory illness on running gait. *J. Athl. Train.* 32(4): 309-314.

Wishart JM, Need AG, Horowitz M, Morris HA, Nordin BE (1995). Effect of age on bone density and bone turnover in men. *Clin. Endocrinol.* (Oxf.) 42(2): 141-146. Abstr.

Index

– V –

– W –

– Z –

Other books by Dr. Phil Maffetone

In Fitness and In Health
David Barmore Productions

Eating for Endurance
David Barmore Productions

Complementary Sports Medicine
textbook, Human Kinetics

The ABCs of Burning Body Fat
David Barmore Productions

The ABCs of Hormonal Stress
David Barmore Productions

The ABCs of Executive Endurance
David Barmore Productions

For information about ordering these books and many

of the products mentioned in this book, including Phil's Bar

and Phil's Shake, contact us at:

Toll-free: (877) 264-2200

E-mail: info@philsbar.com

Web site: www.philsbar.com